MW01601207

In a Split Second

Living with a TBI the Hidden Disability

by Catherine Rosch

DORRANCE
PUBLISHING CO
EST. 1920
PITTSBURGH, PENNSYLVANIA 15238

Dorrance Publishing Co
585 Alpha Drive
Pittsburgh, PA 15238
Visit our website at *www.dorrancebookstore.com*

ISBN: 978-1-4809-9986-2
eISBN: 978-1-4809-9957-2

This book is dedicated to:

George Rosch, who is the most courageous person I know, who has worked so hard to overcome tremendous odds to a find meaningful life again.

Linda Griffith, who had George's back all the way. She believed in him and gave him courage when there wasn't much to be positive about.

Barb Burger, who also had his back. She is showing "New George" the way in his new life, encouraging him not to be afraid, helping him if he falls, and showing him the way to get back up.

Preface

As I sat down to make a scrap book for George a place to put all of his cards, all the emails wishing him well, pictures and articles, I said to myself I'm going to write a book. I had no idea what I was doing but began typing. It just kept coming.

I had so much to say; as I'm writing I found it to be very good therapy for me. I decided that if nothing ever came of it at least I dealt with some of my feeling in our life changing event. As one thought came another one would come. My fingers couldn't keep up with my thoughts. I lot of blood sweat and tears went into writing this book.

Family & friends knew of our life changing journey, but they only knew the surface of what our lives had become. This book deals with this in great detail.

For others that are going through a life changing event I want you to know you can get through this! It can be done it may take every bit of strength you've got, but it can be done!!

This book has taken be almost 3 years to complete. Working full time, a computer crash & my back surgery there were periods of time where this book didn't get touched.

Who Are We

George and I have been happily married for nearly twenty-five years. It is the second marriage for both of us. We love spending time together. Every night at dinner, we spend time talking about our day. If I'm having a bad day, George will try and cheer me up or just simply listen to me vent or offer an, "I'm sorry, hopefully tomorrow will be better." I do the same for him. We are a team.

Over the years, we both have had some major surgeries. We have always been there for the other one. We say, "If it were me helping, you'd do the same for me."

I knew I can count on him as he can count on me.

George is a very strong, proud man. He has some of the best work ethic anyone has ever seen. He takes his job very seriously. More often than not, if he is given a task to do, he will change it up some to make it more effective to get the job done.

George has been a truck driver for nearly thirty-five years. He has driven more than one million plus miles, accident free. He has hauled loads all over the country; he would be gone for weeks at a time. He likes not having to work with anyone, he doesn't like being micro-managed. He knows what he needs to do to get the job done. As he started a family, he came off the road, he found many jobs where he can drive locally. He says, "Driving all over the country was too hard when you have a family." He wants to be home every night.

We love camping. We have had a lot for many years in Wisconsin. We had a beautiful park model. Our plan is to retire there in the summers and be a snowbird, heading south in the winter.

We have a beautiful place with lots of gardens to take care of; every week-end, we would go up to our place to keep our yard groomed and looking its best. We have made some really good friends over the years. After supper, we all gather around the camp fire and tell stories. There is always plenty of laughter to go around! It is such a fun time. We both love it so. It has become our happy place. When I'm stressed, I will go to my happy place. It really does help.

Early 2002

I had gotten really sick, we had to give up our beautiful summer home. It is so hard to do! We are both crying as we say goodbye to the place we have loved so much. The last drive home is a very sad one. (A year after we left the campgrounds, it was sold, and many of our friends left. From what we heard, many things changed, not all for the good. I can look back knowing someone was really looking over us.) There goes our retirement plans.

A few years later

We both miss camping and want to do some traveling. So, we bought a motorhome. We really knew nothing about motorhomes, but it is an adventure we wanted to try; for the most part, we camp close to home.

2006

We decided to take a trip to Branson, Missouri. As we drove into the campgrounds, we couldn't believe what we were seeing, and the gift shop was amazing. The campgrounds were beautiful and clean, I was so excited to get settled in. We wanted to do some exploring. It was like those campgrounds you see on TV. It wasn't campgrounds, it was an RV park. We had so much fun, we went to many shows. One of our favorite shows was the Legend of the Beatles. (As a teenager, I loved the Beatles. I had posters up all over my bedroom, I was a huge Beatle fan.) So, I wanted to see them but wasn't sure they would look or sound like them. Much to my surprise, they looked, talked, and sang just like the real Beatles. As we got up to dance, others soon joined us. I sang to many of the songs, as I knew many of the Beatles songs that were released.

They had a Titanic exhibit; as you were boarding, they gave you a ticket with the name of a real passenger and whether or not they lived or died. They had many Artifex's that have been recovered from the ship. One of the exhibits, you could walk on different levels as the ship was sinking. That was a creepy feeling. There was the grand staircase that was in the movies. It was beautiful.

There were so many things to see, it took us two hours to get through it.

The week went by so fast. So many things to see and do, it is impossible to see everything in one trip. We said we would have to come back to see more.

2008

We took our motorhome, hitting the road, another trip to Branson, Missouri. We had such a fun time the first time, we decided to go back. Three hours into Iowa, we drove into bad weather. We were driving right into a severe storm, there was nothing else we could do but keep going. We finally had to find a place to pull over. George knew we had to park straight into the wind, so we wouldn't rock so much of flip over. I have never been through straight line winds; it was terrifying! Once we could get back on the road, it continued to rain. It was a slow journey. But we finally got there safe and sound.

The gift shop was just as amazing as I remembered it. We got settled in, we decided to take a walk. Much to our surprise, the woods were gone. They were building a new housing development all around the campgrounds. They told us this was the last year for the campground. It, too, was going to be housing. I guess that is progress at its best or worst, depending on who you ask.

We ordered all our tickets for the shows we wanted to see, many of them were different from the first time we had been there. That was fine, it allowed us to see a bunch of new ones.

We decided to go to the Dixie Stampede; it was dinner show. The entire meal was finger food, no silverware. The food was great! Time for the show. The horses were beautiful; the riders did some amazing trick riding. It was a very fun evening.

We also saw the Presley's; this was a family song and dance show. Made up of only family members ranging from four to eighty-nine, everyone had a part in the show. Amazing family of very talented entertainers.

We plan on staying two weeks, but it is springtime. That area of the country can have very dangerous weather in the spring. It won't stop just because we are there. As one storm after another kept hitting the area, we decide to head home. Good thing, too, because the next day, we hear that campground was hit by a tornado. Again, someone is looking out for us.

Hanging on to Life

August 18th, 2011

Our day had begun as any other hot summer day. But at 6:30 AM, George fell off his fuel truck, landing on his head onto the tar hot from the summer heat. The doctors say because he landed on the "soft" tar, his head didn't split open. They say if it had been cement, well, there wouldn't be any need for this story. We are able to put together that George was lying unconscious for about twenty minutes before he came to, trying to figure out what just had happened to him. George wasn't sure of anything at that point but managed to call his boss, who told George to come back to the plant. (Now looking back, how dangerous was that? He could have blacked out again while driving the fully loaded fuel truck). The plant wasn't even close to where he was. George was in at one of his fuel stops, which was about 25 miles away from the plant where he needed to go.

Once George got back to the plant, his boss's boss took over and said, "You are not driving until we know what is going on." He took him over to Urgent Care, who sent him over to North Memorial Hospital.

On the way over to the hospital, George called me at work and told me what happened. I left work immediately. When I got to the hospital, I wasn't sure if I wanted to go into the room, not knowing what I would see or how bad it was. Would he be all bloody? Would his head be split open? To my surprise, there wasn't any blood—nothing really to see. On one hand, this couldn't be too serious; on the hand, I knew he could have a brain bleed. I was scared to death of that. I knew that could take up to six hours to show up.

At this point, they are running scans to make sure there isn't any bleeding in the brain. They are watching him very closely. Time is what he needs at this point. He is being given pain medicine.

After about six hours, we are able to go home. By now, he is very sore, and the bruises are starting to get very colorful.

By the evening, George is very, very sore, but we think he is very lucky. The doctor said that he can't go back to work until Monday. This gives him four days for the bumps and bruises to heal.

The next day (Friday), I had to go back to work. All my co-workers had heard about what has happened. One-by-one as they would come into the office, they asked "How's George?"

I said to my co-workers over and over, "He got lucky." Other than some bumps and bruises, he **seems** to be fine. As I'm saying that, I'm believing it. George has been seriously injured at work before. He always pulls through without even a scratch. But as I'm going to find out, this one is different. As I'm answering the phones and doing my data entry work, I kept thinking to myself about how people die from head injuries just like George's. Enough time had gone by, so I hoped he was out of that woods. I had a vision in my head of what his fall must have been like. How long did it last before he hit the ground? What if he hadn't come to when he did, how long would he have laid there before someone would have found him. All I could think about was the what if's. My mind was going a mile a minute. I don't really remember, but I can venture to say that I didn't get much work done that day.

But, it was Friday, the end of a very long week, I am tired and worried about George. I'm looking forward to the weekend.

Our weekends were always full doing errands, grocery store, bank, and any other errands that filled our weekends. Saturday nights were date nights for us. We would always go somewhere out to eat. We always have plenty to talk about.

George was hurting less by Saturday, he wanted to go get his car. I said to him, "Are you ready for this?"

He said, "Yes," so we went to get this car. This is a long drive from our house. It took us about two to three hours to make the round trip. George was worn out by the time we got home. He laid down to relax; two hours later, he woke up. (I guess he needed to rest).

Sunday has come, and things are beginning to change—not physically, but George didn't want to go back to work. He is showing a great deal of fear, you could see it in his face. He didn't want the doors open. He would say lock it, so no one could get in. He would follow me everywhere I went, he didn't want me out of his sight. He kept saying "I don't want to get back into that truck." He kept repeating that he doesn't want to go back to work. I'm thinking he is afraid to get back into the truck.

We decided to drive him over to see the truck, to face that fear; after all, he makes his living driving trucks. We get there, and he starts crying. By the time we get home, he has started mixing up words. He can't remember what has happened to him.

Monday morning, George is to see the doctor. I can't take him to the appointment, so his daughter, Ashley, takes him. It doesn't take the doctor long to realize that George needs to see a neurologist. Once he gets to the Neurologist office, more tests are conducted, and George and Ashley are told he has a serious traumatic brain injury. I know nothing about traumatic brain injury (TBI) but from that doctor appointment, I would learn a great deal about TBI. In that same split second, two lives would be forever changed.

"Okay," George and I said to the Neurologist. "How long will this take to heal, when can he go back to work? When will he be back to 'normal' (normal, what does it really mean)?" Instead of "normal," we are going to learn the meaning of "the new normal."

The news from the doctor is not good. We have no idea what we are up against, nor have we any idea when he will be able to return to work.

The doctor has said to get plenty of rest, and time would tell what would heal and what wouldn't. We are told to come back in a month. Over the next three years, we will hear, "Come back in a month" and "You can't go back to work."

For next two years, I use my entire vacations on doctor appointments and hospital stays. I'm very grateful to my work for working with me and allowing me to take off as I needed.

The end of September 2011, the doctor sends him to the National Dizzy and Balance Center. George's balance has become so bad that he is falling all the time. They are talking about making him wear a helmet, so as not to injure his head any more than it already has been.

His headaches are like bombs exploding in his head. There is no relief. It never goes away, and nothing seems to help it. As a result of the fall, he now has ringing in his ears. His vision is very poor as well. The Balance Center, we hope, will help with some of the headaches and balance issues.

He goes every day for two weeks. He works very hard with special machines in hopes that it will give him some relief, but it does nothing for him. He continues to fall, his balance is so bad. George used to be able to walk a straight line like no other.

It is so hard for me to watch him continue to go downhill. He knows he isn't as smart as he used to be, and that really bothers him. When will it stop?

Over the next three years, things will continue to get worse for George. Once in a while, he will take one step forward, but it doesn't take long for the two steps backwards to happen. This is common for someone who has suffered a catastrophic injury.

It has now been six weeks since the accident. His fear of people was growing. Some of it is coming from the fact he can't remember what people are telling him. He is terrified of that. It doesn't take long for me to start taking over much of the interaction so as not to stress George. He needs to stay calm. His perception of what people are saying is very often not what they are really saying. He cries like a baby and is so confused. He always says, "Why is everyone being so mean to me?" I would hear the same thing and not get that impression. The words he says makes perfect sense to him but most of the time, they make no sense to anyone else. How do you comfort and help someone while trying to explain to him what was really said so that he could understand it? It is so hard because I sure don't have the answers.

Not the Same Man

October 2011

George was "not" the same man I married. I am holding back the tears. George tries to act "normal" but which "normal," the "new normal" or the old George. It doesn't matter anymore. He can't do either very well. His words won't come out as he intends them to, and he forgets what he has just said.

We are at a company function where there are a few hundred people. George wants so hard to show his co-workers that he is "normal," but he can't do it. The processor is so slow that day, and his words are all mixed up. We have gone on the hay ride several times, and that seems to calm him down.

At the dinner line, there are many choices. George cannot decide what he should have. That is becoming a big problem; he can't make decisions. To avoid stress for George, I just pick out his dinner for him.

By the time we leave, he is very upset. As we go down the road, the tears come. He is convinced that people were talking about him and laughing at him. Truth is no one is even paying any attention to him, but all I can do is hold him and try to comfort him.

George's boss has invited him to come to a safety meeting. George has said that he will go but the night before, the stress had set in, and he couldn't do it. He was too scared to go, afraid he would say the wrong thing and that it would be held against him. He is convinced they were watching him.

George is very seriously injured, that has become very clear, but not enough to make him unaware that he is different. Maybe the emotional pain wouldn't be as bad if he wasn't aware of what was really going on.

November 2011

George has become very depressed. He cries at anything. George's doctor put him on an anti-depressant that helped some with the tears and fears. How do I comfort him? How can I take his pain away? The answer is I can't. In a split second, he goes from being happy to throwing a fit. How do I help him make it better? Truth be told, I can't make it better.

George and Linda at Courage Center it was very peaceful for George

Time to Start the Repairs

December 2011

He is now able to start physical therapy, occupational therapy, and speech therapy. That is where he has met Linda Griffith. She is an expert in brain injuries. She is going fix this and bring back my George. (How silly is that? But I don't know any better.)

All the experts tell us that the brain is an amazing organ, that if the injured part can't be fixed, other parts of the brain will take over. It is going to take time, but George is going to be alright. And you will never know how serious of an injury he had. I have to hang on to that hope for George.

George has found safety in Linda. In his mind, she won't let anything happen to him. His speech therapist Rachel—well, she is from Jersey, need I say more—George is so afraid of her. He likes his physical therapist, Sara. She is nice to him.

He will go to his therapies three days a week for the next eight months. There will be many ups and downs but no matter how many downs there are, George will give it his all. It is just built in George. He wants to get better. We still have a lot of things we want to do.

At one of the early progress meetings we had, George was so afraid to do that meeting that he would only sit between Linda and me. I never did figure out what he was so afraid of because they were all people he knew there. His progress was so slow.

January 2012

George's cognitive test is very low. He has so much trouble figuring things out. He can't follow through with anything. He gets so distracted. I am forever telling him to get back on task. His ability to process anything is very slow. If you would ask him a question, it would take a long time to get an answer. But one of the biggest problems is his coping ability, or the lack of it. How could you send him back into the real work world knowing this? It is beginning to look like George may never be able to go back to work.

If this is the case, now what? We had a plan for saving lots of money in the last ten years of working. All that now is gone in a split second. At this point, I haven't told George about it. He doesn't need that stress, too. So, I carry that by myself.

On to Plan B, I guess—when we barely had a Plan A in place. How am I going to do this? What am I going to do? I have no idea. I had realized early on that our retirement was gone. I am scared to death. I have to be strong for George.

Linda is working with George on the driving machine, but he can't do it; he can't follow or track. He just gets sick. Linda has said that he should put it aside for a while.

Two months have passed; time to try it again, but no luck. Linda works with George about not being able to drive. There are lots of emotions that go into that. This means losing a freedom. He now has to be dependent on others to get around. No one likes to ask for help over and over. George is a very proud man. This is hard. He was used to just getting up and going, but now he has to come to grips with the fact that he can no longer drive.

The neuro-eye specialist Dr. Grosser has said there is just too much optic nerve damage. George has been told that he will never be able to drive again. George has made his living driving, now what?

This is the first of many things that will be taken from George. We both had to deal with the now what. Do we get rid of one of our cars now? Or do we wait for a while in hopes that maybe, just maybe, the doctors are wrong? After all, miracles do happen, right?

The car has sat in the garage for another eight months; after all, if the car is there, it offers hope. Getting rid of the car means it is real. George will never drive again. People say that I should just get rid of it and save on the insurance. It isn't that easy. It isn't about saving money; it is about losing a freedom.

Time to Face Facts Losing Freedom

Early that summer, we start looking at cars online. Should we keep one of our cars and just get rid of one? Which one? We owe on both, and the miles are getting up there. Do we buy new (I have never had a brand-new car), or do we buy used? Why is this so hard, after all, it's just a vehicle? I would give anything if someone could make that decision for me. I guess I just have too much on my plate.

George wants to get a midsize SUV. George has always driven a pickup, so an SUV is smaller but big enough for the grandkids' stuff. In his mind, it is a good compromise. I am leaning towards keeping our Malibu; it only has 68,000 miles on it. We only have a year left to pay. For as far as I have to drive to work, the Malibu gets great mileage. Hmm—get rid of two older vehicles that we still both owed money on or buy one brand new vehicle?

I am willing to look at new, but what kind? Where to buy? I want something that is going to get good mileage and would last for at least ten years or more. That kind of vehicle will have to be foreign. To us, that is a whole other world we have never even considered, foreign. We have always bought American made.

We do lots of homework and decide to look at Honda. I find a Honda CRV, a mid- size SUV, online at RB Honda. That Saturday, we decide to go over to RB Honda and look. That is where we met Kevin DeCaluwe, who is quite frankly the best car salesmen in the car business. He is a caring, honest, sincere person. He listens to our story. He goes with us to test drive the CRV, and we love it. We agree that we should sell both cars for the CRV. But how are we going to get both cars to the dealership? Kevin says that they will come to our house and look at our other car. He said if he liked it and we could put them together, they would take the second car with them that night. We said okay.

Leaving the dealership, we look at each other and say, "Yeah, right, no car salesman does that." We fully believe that we will never hear from him again.

The following Monday, Kevin calls and says that he and a co-worker are on their way to our house. We can't believe what we have just heard. When Kevin get here, he takes our Saturn for a test drive; he likes what he sees. He gives us just what we need to get out of our cars. It is a done deal! We are both so impressed by what Kevin has just done for us. Kevin seems to understand what George is going through. Maybe it is a guy thing about cars. I don't know, but they sure hit it off.

Kevin and his co-worker stay for a while and have some laughs, but it is time to say goodbye to George's freedom. We both walk out to say goodbye to them and thank them so much for going that extra mile.

As they drive away with the car, George realizes some more of his independence is gone. We both just cry and hold each other. It is now real, wasn't it? Oh, yes, it was.

The following Saturday, we bring home our brand new 2012 Honda CRV. For me, this was my first brand new car.

George's therapy is coming along, and each conference is about the same, no really big changes. He is pretty much at MMI (Maximum Medical Improvement) for therapy.

His eye sight isn't improving. Riding in the car or watching a busy show is very difficult for him. He has a really hard time watching TV, so he closes his eyes and just listens. TV is hard for him as his cognitive ability is quite low, and he doesn't understand most of what he is watching or listening to.

George used to love reading things on the computer, but he can no longer do that. His eyes can't track that.

His life consists of therapy three days a week, the other two he just sits and stares all day. Unless I make a list of what to do, he doesn't know what to do. I have to make a calendar for him to shower, shave, and change his underwear.

This is such a dark time for me to watch the smart, funny, full-of-life man that I married be reduced to; this broke my heart.

It is time for the last conference. George decides that he wants to talk this time. Everyone gives their reports. They are about what I expected; his injuries have reached MMI. His physical abilities are shaky at best, his balance continues to be bad, he still falls because sometimes his brain just doesn't send the signal to walk, and down he goes. He has learned to use so-called cheat sheets and his planner to help him function with day-to-day. This helps with some of the cognitive issues but for the most part, he doesn't understand a lot of what goes on around him.

George takes his time to thank every one of his therapists. When it comes to Rachel (the Jersey girl), George tells her, "Thank you. You've helped to not be so afraid." I know that this isn't what speech therapy does, but he says that he is no longer afraid of her! I didn't know he was going to do this. I am so proud of him.

Time for the last day therapy, a day George wishes would never come. He would no longer see his beloved Linda. How is he going to do it without her? Linda has become his everything. She gives him back his life or the tools for him to find his way back. The goodbyes are filled with tears for both of them.

That evening, George just cries. He is scared to death. How is he going to do this thing we call life! He needs to be a valued human being, but so much has been taken away. How is he going to do this?

Not only has Linda made a huge impact on George's life. He says she gave him back his life with her gentleness, her gentle pushing him to be all that he can be. We, too, have made an impact on her. Linda told us that she has seen many patients over her the years, but George's willingness to work hard, even when he struggles, she will always have a special spot in her heart. She will never forget him.

Start of Another Loss

February 2012

George's left leg has started giving way. We have told Dr. Evans (Neurologist). The MRI shows marked cervical and lumbar stenosis. He needs to have surgery right away. If not, he could become paralyzed from the waist down.

We have to get prior authorization from Zurich Insurance Company. Our Qualified Rehabilitation Consultant (QRC) Sharon Kapaska says that she doesn't think they will approve it. She is right. They say it has nothing to do with the fall but rather just age.

I don't know anything about his condition or causes. It is a strenuous time for me to do some research on my own. I learn that yes, it is from aging; however, the numbness in his leg was due to a pinched nerve from the fall.

We jumped through one hoop after another for the next six months. Six months that could have avoided additional damage. His medical insurance doesn't want to pay either because it is from an injury as a result form the fall. Zurich doesn't want to pay because it is from old age. We finally get his medical insurance to agree to the surgery but a week before he is to have the surgery, his medical insurance, again, denies the claim. All I can do is cry. I call the neuro surgeon, who in turn calls the insurance company and gets it all straightened out.

It has become very clear that George will never be able to return to work. We have all known it for a while but have never said it out loud.

Surgery Will Fix It All

August 18th, 2012

George has the first of two surgeries. One year to the day since he has fallen. The doctor feels the neck should be the first one to do. The surgery was long. It seems like it takes forever. The surgery itself goes fine. They fuse his cervical spine. In recovery, he has a hard time coming to. He is very confused. At this point, this was nothing to worry about.

They let Ashley and I go back into the recovery room. They want us to talk to him to help with some of the confusion. I have to be brave, but it is hard; he has no idea who I am. He thinks I am his "other" woman. He keeps telling Ashley, not me, that his "other" woman was there. He says that I would be mad. When we leave the recovery room, all Ashley and I can do is laugh. We laughed so hard, our sides hurt. I think that laughing was just what we needed. In his room, he thinks the doctor is Mickey Mouse. As funny as it may seem, it is also concerning. Why doesn't he know any of us? The doctor says that George will come around but because of his brain injury, it is going to take a long time.

The next day, they try getting George out of bed; he can stand, but he can't walk. His legs won't move no matter how much he tries. He can feel his toes and move them in bed but not walk. All of George's doctors say because of his brain injury, his brain isn't working in that area yet. Because of this, they want to send him to a rehab center instead of coming home.

I am able to get him into the Courage Center inpatient. Both of us are very comfortable with this. After all, George had gotten such great care as out-patient. It is hard leaving him there. Because I have to go back to work and we live so far away, I only go to see him on the weekends. I stop in to pick up his laundry on Friday night, take it home. I hurry to get it washed so I can bring it back on Saturday.

Saturday afternoons are for us. It is fall time, the grounds at Courage Center are filled with gardens. The trees are brilliant oranges, reds, they're so beautiful. Our walks are so special. We take time just to enjoy each other. Sometimes we don't even talk, other times we have plenty to say. Those few hours are time to just let our hair down for a while before we have to start facing our reality.

Sundays are short and sweet; I can't stay long. It, again, is time to start getting ready for my week, to get some house cleaning done.

Rehab Round One

George spends the next eight weeks at the Courage Center, working hard, giving it his all. He has therapy twice a day. Therapy for his neck is in the morning, the afternoon gets him to walk.

George shares a room with man named Gary. Gary is from Rugby, North Dakota. At first, Gary and George got along very well. They are about the same age. Gary had driven a tour bus for a living. Gary had been all over the country as George had driving a truck.

George's throat is very slow to heal. They have to puree all of his food. That blender does some amazingly awful things to food (have you ever seen a T-Bone before and after the blender got done with it?), but it is the only way George can eat.

What is starting to happen is the lack of care by the aids. There is one very large aid that dresses like such a slob. He would come into George's room to gossip and eat. There is another aid that has green hair. She acts like she is stoned all the time. It is not uncommon to wait an hour or so to get someone to answer the call button. I complain but was told over and over again that it is George and Gary, not the staff.

Gary starts raising hell big time. He is a trouble maker. He tells George things like, "The therapists aren't going to help you anymore" or that this was all in George's head and George, in his fragile state, falls into the trap. He calls me one night, so upset. He has had enough. He is checking himself out.

How do you comfort someone that you can't hold or talk to face-to-face? I get him to calm down, or so I think. The next day is Friday. That morning something sets him off right away. He decides right then and there that he is leaving. He is going to walk home. Remember how fragile his mind is.

He has just left. He has started walking with no ID or money; he is so vulnerable. He walks for about three hours, meanwhile the staff realizes he is gone. They search everywhere but can't find him. They even have Linda Griffith looking for him. If anyone can calm him down, she can.

When Linda finds him, he is calm. He says that the walk did him good, and it was a beautiful day for a walk. He has no idea what trouble he has caused. They are very gentle but stern with him.

One day during PT, George falls off the PT table, falling onto the floor. Gary told George that the therapists stood there and watch him fall. Once again, George believes Gary. The funny part about it: Gary isn't even there to see what really happens. But that doesn't matter for Gary. He is determined to make trouble for everyone.

The staff is trying to deal with Gary. They know that he is nothing but trouble. Gary is not only after George but others as well. Everyone at the center is in some sort of fragile state. They are having trouble finding a new place for Gary.

First Homecoming

The day finally comes when George can walk well enough to come home. He is nervous and excited about coming home. I have to go back to work. I had lots of what if's. George is walking pretty good as long as he uses his walker.

We can finally have date night again, but George isn't comfortable with that yet. He is still eating strained food. He doesn't want to be seen in public yet. I am so disappointed, but what can I say? Nothing. Having George back home after two months of being in rehab doesn't mean our life would resume as "normal." The word "normal" is beginning to wear many different hats. I'm as confused and afraid as I've ever been.

George may have physically come home, but he is very different than before he went in for his first surgery. I don't have any time to feel sorry for myself. He is so vulnerable that I don't have time for my feelings. My job taking care of George has to change pretty much every day. I need to protect and take care of him. Every day is a new challenge, far as his needs go. Some days he remembers what he has learned, he can apply it to his task, but some days I have to take care of him because he doesn't remember how or what to do.

As I look back at it now, I didn't realize how many more times I would have to change to make room for that "new normal." I don't think I really always like that "new normal." He scares me. I don't always know how to deal with him. Where is my "old George"? I miss him so!

I am glad to have him home! But as much as I don't like him being gone, I have gotten used to being home alone. It kind of became my sanctuary, my place of peace. Now, I have to get used to having George home again. I have to take care of him, worry about him, and make sure he gets what he needs. He is so fragile and vulnerable.

George, too, is glad to be home, but he is used to us being apart. In some ways, we have to get used to each other again.

As much as he hates the Courage Center, it has become a safety net for him. Now, he has to do things for himself.

Every morning before I leave for work, I make sure his lunch is ready. I make a list for him: what time to eat and what time to take his medicine. I won't let him go upstairs unless I am home. At night, I help him get showered. He sleeps a lot. That is what his body needs to heal.

After a few weeks at home, eating starts to be a little easier. I don't have to blend everything to death. But now he discovers that food doesn't taste like he remembers it tasting (one more thing he lost). He no longer likes food that he loved before the accident. It is a challenge to know what he will like. Even more of a challenge: he may like it this time but not the next time.

It is four weeks after he had arrived home before he could eat well enough for date night. I think it is one of the best dates I have ever been on. George does it, but boy, he was tired when we got home.

George continues to improve over the next six weeks. He is getting stronger. He has another surgery facing him before the end of the year. We see the neuro surgeon right after Thanksgiving. The surgeon says that George is finally strong enough to do the second surgery. One thing the doctor does say is that this is a **very painful surgery**. Boy, is he right. I've never seen George hurt so much.

Cathy and Ashley

This Surgery Will fix the problem Right?

December 20th, 2012, surgery day.
Ashley and I were both there. The surgery began very early in the morning. We said our goodbyes. I told George not to be afraid, that I was with him. I was so scarred, but I couldn't let him see that. I had to be strong for him. After George went into surgery, Ashley and I went down to get some breakfast. I was so scared that I ate until I was about to explode.

We waited another six hours before the doctor came out. Do you have any idea how long six hours can be when you're waiting for news from the doctor? Let me tell you, it was long! People came and went from the waiting room. A new group would come and go. I didn't think it would ever end. Then it did. The doctor came out to tell us how it went. He said George had lost a lot of blood, but they were able to recycle his own blood. I wasn't exactly what he meant by that. (I remember thinking and laughing to myself. Did they suck it up off the floor and put it back where it came from? Where does lost blood go?). He said it was a hard surgery, but George came through it. Now we wait. I thought to myself, *wait for what?* It wasn't until days, or really even weeks later, did I know what he meant.

George was in recovery for a long time. Again, his brain injury; the slow processor wouldn't allow him to come to. It seemed like the knockout drugs would damage the brain even more with every time he had surgery. So, now he not only had to recover from the surgery itself, but his brain would have to boot itself back on track. So, now we wait. How long? No one knew. In time he might improve, but there may be no change ever. There was nothing anyone could do except wait for George's processer to turn on. Every time George has surgery, it takes more and more from him, he recovers less and less.

First day after surgery was very scary. George's speech was very slurred. When they sat him up in bed, he leaned to the right, almost to the point he was tipping over. I told him to sit up straight; he said he was. I was concerned that he might have had a stroke. The doctors noticed this, too. They told George to sit up straight. Again, he said he was. They didn't seem to be too concerned about it. They just said, "Give it a day or so."

Okay, what do I know about this stuff after all?

They are the doctors. They know what is best, right? They are the highly trained experts. I look back on it a lot and wonder if the outcome would have been different if I had only…? Hind sight is a wonderful tool but only for the future.

George's back brace didn't fit well, but they didn't want him walking without it. So, he had to be refitted. What should have taken a couple of hours to get corrected took an entire day. I guess that full day in bed was good for him. He needed the rest.

Day two after surgery was a pretty good day. He finally got his back brace. He wanted to try to walk. He was still in such extreme pain but wanted to walk, even if it meant just a few steps. It took two nurses to get him out of bed and stand him with his walker. He was able to make it to the door of his room and back. Pretty darn good considering what he had just been through.

Day three started out fine. George went for a walk a little farther than the day before. He did well. Time for lunch, then a walk. But the next walk was different. It took four nurses to get him just to stand up. It just didn't seem to work. His processing didn't seem to be working. He finally took a step and then two. He managed to get to the hall where he just collapsed. It's a good thing he had a nurse on either side of him. The doctors didn't seem to be too concerned, considering what he had just gone through and the amount of pain he was in.

Okay, I will go with what they say. After all, they are the experts, right?

The decision was made that he would again have to go to rehab. He needed time to heal and get stronger. I was okay with that because I knew I couldn't take care of him or leave him alone yet. Again, I had to decide what rehab center. The only one I knew anything about was Courage Center. After his last experience there, I didn't really want him to go back. So, when they told me the Courage Center was full, I wasn't too upset. That meant sending him to a nursing home. Oh my God, I wasn't ready for that, but what choice did I have? I told the social worker that I wanted a nice, clean place. He suggested Good Samaritan Ambassador. I remember thinking to myself that any place named the Ambassador had to be good. As it turned out, that thought didn't let me down at all.

Rehab Round Two

December 23rd, 2012

George arrived at the Good Samaritan Ambassador. It was very late that afternoon and very cold. The parking lot was close to the door, and I didn't have to pay for parking. So far so good. It was one level, kind of small compared to some of the nursing homes I had seen before. I walked in the door with suitcase in hand, ready to go. The place didn't stink like some nursing homes do. Someone met me. They took me to his room. It seemed like the longest walk ever. The place was decorated so nicely for Christmas. I was glad because I knew that this was where we were going to spend Christmas.

I walked into his room. I was amazed it was a beautiful private room with refrigerator and microwave. Modern, up-to-date, decorated very nicely, two big windows to look outside and not a rooftop like at the hospital. Oh, and cable—that was a treat for us because we didn't have cable at home!

I got there before he did, so I was able to get him unpacked. He arrived and said the same thing. "This doesn't look like or smell like your typical nursing home. So far, so good."

The nurse came in to greet him and get him settled. It was time to get the paperwork out of the way, that took a while. When we were finished, the nurse stayed and visited for a bit.

By now, it was the evening (darkness had set in it), a cold winter night. I was so tired, all I wanted to do was to go home and go to bed, but George didn't want me to go. He was afraid to stay there by himself. He liked the place, but it wasn't home—strange people. George was very tired, in a lot of pain, and so I stayed for another couple of hours. I got George to settle down. I helped him get washed up and ready for bed. It took him a while to get to sleep. Once he was asleep, I left. I had a 40-minute drive home.

He was up many times that night; the pain was unbearable. It was hard for him to make it from one dose of pain medication to the next. He was having such hard time with pain control. No matter what he did, nothing seemed to help. He would go from sitting up, to lying down with ice.

December 24th, 2012, Christmas Eve.

George called me very early that morning. I missed him so. Carrying on a conversation with him was hard because he was so drugged. I felt so alone. Because his surgery was so close to Christmas, we all knew that George wouldn't be able to come to Christmas. So, we all decided to bring Christmas to him, wherever he was. We all tried to make the best of it. What else could we do? Now even our Christmas was all ruffled up. Merry Christmas…?

I was going over to my sister's home for my family Christmas about 4:30 PM, so that morning before I went to spend time with George, I got the food that I was bringing, ready to go. I got over to see George about 11:00 AM. Ashley had also come to spend some time with him. She didn't have to be to work until 5:00PM. George slept off and on the whole time we were there. She and I walked around visiting with anyone that would talk to us. It seems like that is all she and I had been doing since the morning of his first surgery.

It was time for me to go. We said our goodbyes, but he didn't even really know that anyone was even there.

When I left, I had to go pick up my dad before going over to my sisters. It was cold and getting dark, but Santa Claus was coming!

When we got to Nancy's, I had to help my dad to the door. I got him in, and I then went back to get the food. I was about to climb the stairs, food in hand, when my phone rang; it was the nursing home. George had fallen and couldn't get up, so they called 911. It was determined that he should go to the hospital. I said I would meet them there.

For whatever reason, George was trying to get out of bed. His socks didn't have grips on them, he slid down the side of the bed, hitting his head, and landing with his head under the bed. I'm pretty sure you couldn't do that if you tried. How in world did he?

Oh God, what about our dinner? How will Dad get home? We decided that my nephew, Tony, would bring Dad home. Nancy would keep the food, and we would do Christmas the next day, if George was alright.

On the way to the hospital, I called Ashley, and she met me at the hospital. Being Christmas Eve, there was no one anywhere. I have never seen the hospital so empty. I mean, not a soul in the hallways. I guess when it comes to Christmas, sick people don't count. Christmas dinners with family and friends must go on in hopes that Santa Claus will soon be there.

George was in so much pain, so they kept giving more pain meds. He was so out of it at that point; he forgot to breath and then the alarms went off.

Ashley and I were terrified. Not knowing is the worst! They took him down for an MRI. The MRI didn't show any damage, so it was decided that he could go back to the nursing home.

Now just because the hospitals are empty, seemingly not busy, that is not true for the ambulances and Emergency Medical Techs (EMT's). We waited, for what seemed to be forever, for them to come back and get him.

By the time we got back to the nursing home, it was after 11:00 PM. We hadn't eaten and were starving. Ashley was going to stop to pick up something for us. Forgetting it was Christmas Eve, nothing was open except for McDonald's. I don't like McDonald's, but I was too hungry to care. By the time I got George settled down and I got home, it was almost 1:00 AM. Poor Cody needed to go out. He hadn't eaten. I was so wound up, it was about 3:00 AM before I got to sleep. What a Christmas Eve. I was so, so sad. I just held Cody and cried.

Four hours later, the phone rang, and it was George. He was just crying, He was in so much pain but at the same time, so out of it, he would forget to talk. Well, Merry Christmas! I didn't know how much more of this I could take. He needed me, and I knew this, but I was so tired. I didn't know what I could do to make it better for him. I felt so bad for him. *Please, someone fix it for me and George.*

I went to see George about 12:00 PM. To my surprise, Jaelyn and Ashley were already there. Jaelyn, our granddaughter, had a pretty dress on. She wanted to look nice for Grandpa. We all tried to make something of Christmas, as hard as it was. Jaelyn wouldn't get to open her Christmas presents until that April. George and I never did open our cards. We just held them for the next year. George was on a lot pain meds, so he slept pretty much through Christmas.

I left about 3:00 PM to go get Dad so we could, again, try Christmas dinner at Nancy's. We made it, and dinner tasted so good. Now, I don't know why that Christmas dinner tasted so good. After all, it was on its second of cooking. I think it was one of the best Christmas dinner's I've ever had. It was nice to just sit for a bit. I got home about 7:00 PM that evening. It was time for me to get ready for work the next day. I was so tired that I went to bed early.

George continued to be in so much pain. They were trying so many different things to control the pain. Nothing was working. He had physical therapy twice a day but he was so doped up, he would fall asleep on the machines. They would continue to get George walking, and sometimes he could go a few feet with two people helping; sometimes right out of the get go, his legs wouldn't go, or they would collapse.

The MRI looked good after his fall, but no one could seem to figure out why he couldn't walk. Why was he still in so much pain? They were giving him so many pain meds, he was so dopey and had no idea who he was or anyone else for that matter.

January 1st, 2013, a New Year, a New Start!

Oh, I so hoped that was true! I couldn't take another year like 2012. The only thing I really knew for sure was that it was a new year.

It was tradition that on New Year's Eve and New Year's Day, we always had lots of snacks/junk food and watched movies. I had been so concerned about George that I forgot all about it.

I was at the nursing home on New Year's Day with George when we got surprise visitors. It was Debbie and Paul; they said they were bringing New Year's tradition to us. I thought, *how nice*. George was so out of it, but Paul tried to make conversation with him. He was just too drugged, but the three of us had a nice visit. George didn't even know they were there or when they left. I remember thinking that when they left, I felt like I was all alone and that I had better get used to it. George was there in body only. Later that day, Nancy came to visit, but George didn't even know she had been there.

Friday night, January 4th, 2013

George couldn't stand it anymore. The nursing home called our doctor. It was decided to send him to the hospital. Another call to Ashley, another long night of waiting for some answers. It was a Friday in the waiting room at the hospital, it was full of people coughing, crying, and yes, bleeding. What a creepy, sad place. Doctors ordered more tests, more blood work, and another MRI. This time, they admitted him. Once he got in his room, he fell asleep, so we left.

The next day, we all had a meeting with Dr. Stuart (AKA Mickey Mouse). He was going to try putting him on a medication for diabetic nerve pain. He said it would take a bit to get it adjusted just right for him. He said the pain was coming from the nerve damage. It made sense. Someone was finally trying to help George. God knows the surgeon wasn't; all he wanted to do was over-drug him with pain meds.

George was able to get about six hours of rest that day. I just let him sleep. The next morning, he seemed to be a little clearer in his thinking. He seemed to be in a little less pain; now, that may have been wishful thinking on my part—I don't know. Dr. Stuart had reduced some of his pain meds and had him taking the Gabapentin four times a day.

Sunday, he was able to go back to the nursing home. It was late afternoon before he got back there to the rehab center, early evening before I would leave.

I finally got home about 8:00 PM. I had to feed Cody, take him outside, then we spent some time together. I told Cody how his dad was hurting so much, and there wasn't anything either he or I could do to help except be there to comfort him. As I looked into Cody's big beautiful eyes, I felt as if he was telling me that everything was going to be alright. For that brief moment, I felt an inter peace. Cody was truly our little "Love Bug," with that, I started to get ready for another long week. Monday morning will come only soon.

Work had become a place for me where I could forget a bit about George and let myself relax. Knowing he was safe and being taken care of.

Over the next couple of weeks, George was out of it more and more. He seemed to be living in a fog. Sometimes his pain was an eight instead of a ten, but that wasn't really saying much. When people would come visit him, most of the time he had no idea anyone had even been there. The only person George remembered coming regular was Rose (George's sister) because she always brought him Christmas cookies. He wouldn't always remember what they talked about, but he remembered who brought the cookies.

They decided to do his therapy once a day instead of twice a day. The thinking was, maybe they were pushing his walking to fast. George continued to fall asleep in therapy. His progress was so slow, but true to George's form, he wasn't giving up.

He was making friends with the therapist. Chris, his occupational therapist, was good to George. He had George's back much like Linda Griffith did.

George and Chris would joke a lot, but George knew Chris wouldn't let anything happen to him. George was working so hard to get strong and better.

Funny how Chris could joke around with George while in therapy. George could even joke back with Chris. Somehow George knew it was safe. Chris was the only one that could do this. If others tried, George would get all upset not understanding it at all, thinking people were being mean to him.

Better, what does that really mean anyway?

January 23rd, 2013, George's birthday

His birthday was on a Thursday. I wanted to spend some time with my love. I got there shortly after work. I walked in his room. He was sitting in his big chair, so far out in space. I said hi to him, and he didn't even know who I was. I wanted to give him a birthday kiss, but he was afraid of me, I could see the fear in his face, that scared look of someone is going to harm me, and I can't do anything to help himself. I stayed for just a bit because it was very clear that I made him nervous. I didn't even make it to the hall before I started to cry.

Is he ever going to know who I am? Is this now another "new" George? One who is afraid of his wife, his best friend in the world? I don't think I can do this. My adult mind understands what just happened, but my emotions sure don't!

People were in and out all day. It was a very bad pain day, so he was very doped up. Many family and friends brought him cakes. He was so out of it that day. I was like, you ring the door bell, but no one was home. He just didn't have a clue.

The nursing home brought him a cake; I thought that was such a nice jester. I'm so glad he was able to be at Good Samaritan. They took such good care of him.

I went back the next day. This time he knew who I was, but he was still out of it. He asked me where all the cakes came from. He had no idea anyone was there at all. He didn't know it was his birthday.

Thoughts were flying around in my head. Would George ever get strong enough to come home? By now, we knew he could never work again. That didn't seem to bother him because he didn't even know what work was. He wasn't really functioning. He really didn't know much of anything. People would tell him stuff and receive a blank stare.

I knew he couldn't come home like that. I couldn't take care of him; I work to support us. I was so afraid. *What should I to do with him?* I wanted him to be well taken care of. *Where ever he would go? Could he just stay where he was at?* After all that had become his home, he felt safe there. For the most part, I had lost my husband, my best friend. I knew he would need full-time care.

That was a definite low spot! I kept thinking, *how much more can this poor guy take, or me for that matter?*

Things Started to Change

Saturday, George was less in a fog. He could understand simple commands. He couldn't carry on a conversation yet, but there was some slight improvement.

He didn't seem to be in so much pain; might the Gabapentin be starting to work? Yes, in fact, it was!

They were able to start reducing his pain medication a little bit. In doing so, he wasn't in such of a fog, but he had lost a lot of his cognitive ability. He needed to use his brain to make it work and think again. If he had hope of leading any kind of a life, he had to get that brain stimulated.

I remembered some of the stuff that Linda had taught him.

I brought him the check book and helped him pay two bills. It was very slow, so hard for him to do (I pictured the wheels in his brain moving so slow, kind of like the Tin Man in the Wizard of Oz. Those wheels were so rusty). We took it one step at a time. He couldn't ask me what was next because he didn't know what to ask. As he would finish each step, I would tell/show him what to do. It took two hours for him to pay bills and then balance the check book. But he did it, and it was done right! I was so excited, he was so tired.

Jaelyn is working with Grandpa playing Cootie—rules were always according to Jaelyn.

There is Hope, I thought to Myself!

I brought all of our games, and I asked everyone in the nursing home to play games with him or card games that he learned in therapy. We all helped, especially Jaelyn. At first, it was extremely hard for George.

Jaelyn and Grandpa played Memory over and over to help him. She would come every Tuesday (it became Grandpa Tuesday) If Grandpa was having trouble she would tell him; think hard Grandpa I know you can do it!!

Early on, Jaelyn was the one that worked with Grandpa, playing endless games of memory with him. She would tell Grandpa, "Keep trying, Grandpa. You can do it. Grandpa, how are you feeling today?" One time when she was visiting him, she told Grandpa that it didn't matter if he couldn't walk, she loved him no matter what. If there ever was a prescription for five-year-old granddaughter, she was it. She somehow had the touch that he so desperately needed.

As they continued to reduce George's pain medications to where he could function, along with everyone's help, his cognitive ability was starting to get a "little" sharper. Progress was slow, and not every day was a good one. But there was hope! I remember thinking, *baby steps*. However, as little as the steps were, they were, for the most part, moving forward rather than always backwards.

They started working at building up George's upper body strength. That seemed to be the only part of his body that he had control of. Walking was just not working; sometimes all he had to do was stand and down he would go but other times, could walk twenty feet or more. However, you never knew which time it was going to be, that was the problem.

George was forming a bond with Chris. He felt very safe at the nursing home. He was beginning to think of it as home. By now, he was heading into his third month there. I was becoming comfortable at home without George. *Was this going to be our new lives? Was this maybe the best place to leave George?* Believe me, this thought has crossed my mind many times.

George continued to work as hard as he could. George and Chris were beginning to face facts (but I wasn't being kept in the loop). They talked about what would happen if he couldn't walk anymore. They started working on learning how to transfer, building up the upper body.

Over the next few weeks, he went to therapy every day. He worked as hard as he could. They stopped trying to walk; it was becoming too risky. George could not afford to fall and hit his head. The fog was beginning to lift as he was able to reduce the amount of pain meds. His pain level was down to five or six.

Funny, I remember thinking, *five-six is still a lot of pain but where George has been, five-six is doable. It's all relative, I guess.*

Even though he was able to reduce his pain meds, that wasn't really saying much. But he was able to function a bit more—at least know what was going on around him some of the time. For short periods of time, we played games, and he understood them—some days. Every day was different, some better than others.

He was getting better. He just had such a long way to go, but he had come so far from where he was. He needed to learn how to dress himself, to recite his name and address, just everyday basic things that we all take for granted.

Time to Face Facts

Sometime in mid-February

It was time for a doctor appointment with the neuro surgeon. Keep in mind, we had not seen him since the last surgery. We kept asking if we should come in, but he would just call orders in to the nursing home. Finally, the nursing home said it was time to go, regardless of what they said.

At that appointment, x-rays showed everything was good. The surgeon's assistant said, "Everything was coming along fine."

"What?" I asked. "How can you say that? He can't walk. He is still in so much pain. It was our family doctor that cared enough to put him on Gabapentin to help with some of the nerve pain."

I didn't mean to go off on him, but he was in such a hurry to get us in and out of there. I wondered why the hurry; did they have something to hide? We hadn't even seen the surgeon but rather his assistant, who was the biggest smart ass I've come across in a very long time. He was so flip and uncaring. He told us give it time and come back in two months. Looking back at it, we believed that something went wrong in surgery. At that visit, George asked the assistant why he couldn't walk.

The assistant said it was possible that there was a nicked nerve that could explain why he can't walk.

We were rushed out of that office so fast. They just didn't care about George but rather would we file a suit against them. Of course, we should have, but we just couldn't take on another thing. George just didn't have it in him. I felt (and still feel) we should have, if for no other reason than that surgeons just can't do that to someone and get away with it.

I remember the ride back to the nursing home; I was so mad and upset.

After all George has been through, how could some young, smart-mouth punk treat him like that?

The next week was time for a care conference at the nursing home. I was excited to hear what everyone had to say with George's progress. I thought he was doing so well from where he had come from.

Our meeting was for 1:30 PM. Ashley, Jaelyn, and I sat on one side of the table. George sat next to Chris. Chris had become the "new" Linda. He felt very safe with him. I think even safer than with me.

Time for the meeting to start. I had talked to a lot of the people that were there but never face to face. (I had done a lot of communications by email and phone). We went around and introduced ourselves.

"The reason I called this meeting," the social worker said, "was to explain where George is now and what we hope for his future." The social worker continued, "George has worked so hard to fight back from where he was. He has given it his all. We have so enjoyed working with him. He has done everything we've asked of him. It's not very often we see someone work so hard."

That Being Said

Chris was first; he looked at George and then at me. He said, "George isn't going to walk again. We've been trying and trying. George and I decided it was too dangerous to risk falls. There was so much nerve damage, and the brain isn't always sending signals to walk. The goals all along has been to get George to be the best that he could be—whatever that is."

I thought I was going to throw up right then and there. I almost had to leave the room. I had just heard the worst news I had ever heard; oh, but wait, there was more. Next up was the head nurse; she said that George would be in a great deal of pain for the rest of his life. The hope was to get him down to a "five" with strong pain meds. That would be on a "good" day. The good news was that his cognitive ability was improving from the low point. All our hard work with George is paying off to take him from not understanding most of what said to him and that blank stare, to be able to understand much of what we say to him. As they're talking, I'm thinking, *what kind of life is this?*

They all said that George had reached medical maximum improvement. The plan going forward would be to send George home with his own wheelchair. He would now continue his physical therapy at home. A home healthcare team would come in to teach George how to bath himself and be as independent as he could be.

As we left the meeting, I just wanted to run away. I just felt sick. I couldn't stay; I had to go home. George was accepting of this, but he already knew about it; I didn't. I had no idea. I had been broadsided with the worst news ever. I felt so alone. *Why hadn't anyone kept me in the loop?*

By time I got home, it was dark out. I picked up Cody, gave him big hugs. I began to cry for hours. I wasn't sure if I was mad at Chris or just felt so bad for George. After all, he was the one going through it, not me. Oh, but in fact, I was going through it, just like George was. My pain was just different.

I so needed hugs from "old George," for him to tell me it will be okay. But "new George" didn't know how to do that sort of thing.

There Was No Time
to Feel Sorry for Myself

Chris, along with his team, had to come out to our house to do a home evaluation. And to see what things I had to change before it was safe enough for George to come home. They went over everything with us (meaning me) making suggestions along the way. These would all have to be done before he could come home. So, time was not on my side.

I had to get a two-inch-high ramp for the back door; I had no idea where even to begin. *Where do I start to look for a ramp for someone in a wheel chair?* I decided to do as I always do. I Googled it. I typed in "two-inch ramp" and up came lots of information. I spent one entire evening looking for this and emailing those that I could get more information on. Next night, I read through all my emails, along with all the information I had gathered. I had talked to this place. They answered my questions, and they understood my time frame. Time to make a decision; I took a chance and ordered it. The ramp came in about seven days. I took it out of the box; it was exactly what I needed. I was pretty proud of myself.

One checked off the list. On to the next. I thought to myself I *CAN do this, on to the next one*.

I had to put in safety bars in our bathroom, get a special seat for the shower, grab bars for his toilet. Those all had to be in place before he could come home.

It took me a couple of weeks to get this all done, but I did it. What a production to get this to work. We had three bathrooms, I would now have to shower upstairs, so we could keep George's shower set up the way he needed it to be. But rather than moving all my bathroom stuff upstairs, I just showered upstairs and came down for the rest of my bathroom use. George would shower in one bathroom and use the toilet in another bathroom. It was a production for both of us, but it was the only way it would work. To say our house was not handicapped ready was an understatement. But we made it work.

In the meantime, Chris and George were wrapping things up in therapy. His cognitive ability was as good as it was going to get…I guess.

Time to Come Home

After nearly four months in rehab, it was time for George to come home, time to start another chapter in this journey. Saying goodbye was sad, we had made a lot of new friends there.

It had become a safe haven—home for George. That was the only home George now remembered as home. So, to say he was going "home," in his mind, he was going to *my* home, not George's. That being said, he was pretty much terrified of "*going home.*"

Time to load up and go. I got George into the car and realized I didn't know what to do with the wheelchair. I didn't even know that it folded up. Boy, did I have a lot to learn.

This might be harder than I think.

It was happy/sad; it is scary for both of us. We had been apart from each other for so long. That first day home was rough! We didn't know how to act around each other anymore. George was right, my home was no longer his home. We didn't know how to act around each other or talk to each other anymore. We were *home* for a couple of hours when George began to cry. He wanted to go back home. Maybe he didn't belong here anymore. Our house was no longer his home. He didn't feel safe there. He didn't know how to take care of himself or what to do with me. He was so scared. I felt so bad for him! What could I do to help him? All I could do is be there for him and hold him when he was scared. I told him we would take it one day at a time together. We would get through this. At that point, I didn't know how we were going to get through this, but we had to somehow, someway.

How do I take care of someone who is in a wheelchair? Are there signs that something is wrong? Would he, in time, ever improve? Are we done with doctors? Now what, are we just thrown out there, expecting to go on with our lives like nothing had ever happened? Because something is wrong, and something has changed.

It was my job to take care of George. I sure wish George had come home with a how-to manual on how to do this so-called life after a catastrophic injury. I was as scarred as he was. I didn't have that magic manual that makes things all right. There was no how-to-do-this manual. I guess I needed to listen to what I was telling George. One step at a time!

Somehow our little Cody knew what to do with George. He would cuddle with him. George was much more relaxed when Cody was around. Funny, they hadn't see each other in almost four months. Cody brought us back together. We had something to think about other than this so-called life. Cody made us laugh, and he made George feel very safe. I guess Cody was the how-to manual.

Sunday, day 2 home

For me, I had to get laundry done and try to do the normal stuff to get ready to start my week. George did a lot of resting that day. Our worlds only seem to come together when it involved Cody.

That afternoon, George and I talked some about what was next. Home healthcare was next and more physical therapy at home. He was afraid to have people in if I wasn't there.

Monday came again. Work had become my break from George and my home life that was so out of control. I called the home healthcare nurse. I told her how afraid he was; she agreed that it would be a good idea for the first few visits I should be there. So, she came after I got home from work.

The first meeting, she brought the team that would be working with George; this way George could meet them with me there. Everyone was nice, and George felt comfortable with them.

The nurse would come three days a week; she got his meds set for him for the week. She also did vitals and worked on feelings with him. She set up everything for him.

Physical therapist would come in every day. They continued to work on stuff that Chris was doing with George.

The bathing nurse would come in three days a week. She taught him how to bathe himself.

I felt bad that life had come to having complete stranger teach George how to bathe himself, but it had. If he was going to get to be independent, this had to be done.

All of this help was a huge relief for me. I knew he was safe learning to be independent. I wouldn't have been able to keep working and take care of George if we hadn't had this help.

This kept his days very busy. He worked very hard, and he was very tired at night. Rest is also very important for him. None of this was easy for George and with the brain injury, it was even harder.

Progress was very slow. He called me (with the help of his occupational therapist) one day at work. He said he had a surprise for me. He was so excited; he said I had to wait until I got go home. I couldn't imagine what it was. When I got home that night, he couldn't wait to show me that he had learned in occupational therapy that day. He learned to use the microwave from his chair. He was so proud of himself! After all that he lost and that had been taken away from him over the last couple of years, he could now use the microwave by himself. His first step at returning independence—funny how something so small could be so huge.

His walking just wasn't coming along at all. With my help, he did all of his exercises (believe me, if I hadn't pushed him hard, he wouldn't have done his exercises). Some days worked better than others. It just wouldn't get good enough to say he was walking. Nothing ever seemed to change as far as walking; the damage was just too severe. He decided he had enough. I agreed. After all, it had only been four months since his surgery. That was a sad day. I knew it was true, but George just needed a break from all therapies. He wasn't giving up but at the same time, he was beginning to realize this might be it.

For the next six weeks, George did nothing but stare into space. He loved sitting outside; it gave him an inner peace. He would sit outside for many hours every day. He was starting to crawl back in his shell.

Good Samaritan had sent him an invitation to a rehab brunch. He decided to go, and he was excited to go. That night he said he had a really nice time; it was good to see friends that he hadn't seen in a while. Going back to Good Samaritan was like going home. It was a place that was safe for George. He couldn't get hurt anymore.

At the breakfast in walked Barb Burger who would be come the new Linda Griffith. They talked about volunteering and what are some of the things George could do to help around there. They are always in need of someone to play games with the residents or just someone to talk to. On the ride home, he told me that he was going to talk to Good Samaritan about volunteering. I was really excited for him. It was something he could do. He started with just two days a week. He wanted to give something back. We didn't know it at the time, but this was now his purpose in life. Giving back to those in need of putting their lives back together. Who better than George.

George and Barb

Barb recalled when she first met George; he was depressed. He could not figure out why he didn't die. He wished he could die rather than living life in a wheel chair. He was very angry! She and George talked during the rehab brunch; she explained to him that God has a purpose for him, that is why he is still living. George needed to figure out that purpose. His life will drastically take a turn from what he was used to, but he needed to open his heart and be open to this new world.

Barb explained that the timing is strange because Good Samaritan was looking for someone like him to visit other rehab patients to help them with their recovery. They needed someone that has the experience of being a resident, someone who knows the ropes, the ups and downs. Someone that can relate to their pain, both physical and emotionally. George thought about it for a minute, then explained that maybe he could do that but still not confident that he could make a difference to someone.

She asked him, "What else are you going to do besides feel sorry for yourself? If this didn't work out, you could just stop volunteering. So, what have you got to lose?"

George agreed.

His weeks were kept busy. Three days a week, he would go to the Courage Center and two days a week, he would volunteer at Good Samaritan. The first couple of weeks, he still struggled; he could not see the difference in what he was doing, he felt he made no impact to others.

Barb talked him into giving it some time. She reassured him that she would have his back.

He was still so angry with his life. He had to force a smile. Barb recalls that the staff had a hard time relating to him because he wasn't ready to take any in as friends. In some ways, he was trapped. He couldn't go anywhere without a major production. Transportation was very hard to line up because we lived out so far.

It was time to see the neurologist that visits; we asked about more physical therapy. The doctor thought this would be good for George. So, back to Courage Center he went, three days a week. It was there he met Brooke, who would become the new Linda Griffith. Brooke was gentle with him but made him work.

To get to the Courage Center, he would have to take two different buses. It took him two hours, one way to get there. I picked him up after work. So, for three days a week, he would spend at least two hours a day getting to the Courage Center. He would take the bus from Rogers (where we lived) to Maple Grove community center and very often have an hour layover. To the Courage Center, it was about a 30-mile trip. He couldn't relax because he was so afraid of missing the second bus. He was so afraid of getting lost. (This coming from a man that made his living driving all over the country. And knowing how and where to go) And how would he get home? Where was home? We would go over what he should do if he missed the bus. He had his cell phone that I put important numbers in. (However, that was a waste of my time. He didn't know how to use a cell phone) At all times he had his identification, along with bus identification on him. I also put my phone numbers in his bag. How could he do anything? He couldn't even figure out what to do if he got lost. So much had been taken from him. Those three days a week were very nerve racking for me knowing that he didn't really know what to do in an emergency. As much as we went over it, if it came down to it, would he be able to get to me or home? More than likely not but thankfully, we never had to put it to the test.

Therapy lasted for eight weeks with very little improvement, if any. We all knew that he once again had reached medical maximum improvement or MMI. But in those eight weeks, he had become so attached to Brooke. He could talk to her. He was still pondering his life and what he should now do with it. He needed a purpose. Who was he? What could he now do with his life? He still wanted to have meaning in his life. But what?

He could no longer walk, a great deal of his eye sight was gone, every second of every day he had ringing in his ears. A man who once was very strong and proud is now a confused, scared man. His short-term memory area was severely damaged from the fall. He would ask what was on TV and no more than ten seconds later, would ask again what was on TV. It was very common for him to repeat the same question many times in any given evening. He processed things very slowly. His perception was no longer the same. If someone said something to him that may be something that you or I could just blow off and move on. He couldn't do that; he took everything to heart, and his feelings got so hurt. He didn't know how to love me anymore. Life was so hard for him.

George was very seriously injured both physically and mentally. But not enough to not know what was really going on. That is what hurts so much! He would have been better off not knowing anything. I think he would be happier.

One day when we were leaving for the doctor, I asked him if he could get one thing from his injury back, what would it be?

He thought for a couple of minutes and then said, "Take his brain injury away."

I was shocked, I thought for sure he would say, "to walk again."

I know my husband very well. We think so much alike that I thought for sure he would want to walk again. I guess I didn't know "the new George" as well as I thought. I thought about his answer very hard and realized that if his brain injury went away, the other injuries would go away, too. Pretty smart thinking for someone that has lost so much! I knew at that point "my George" was still in there somewhere.

The last day with Brooke was very emotional, lots of tears. The ride home that night was very long and full of tears. I felt so bad for him. I wasn't the one that could take his hurt away. He felt so alone. He was so afraid and searching so hard for some meaning in his life.

In some ways, I had a hard time understanding his need for meaning in his life. And what did that really mean anyway? I sure didn't know. After all, I got up every day, went to work, came home, and took care of him. My life was more than full. He was always very helpful around the house. If he saw something that needed doing, he did it, no questions asked. He would cook dinner because he was home first and didn't want to eat at 7:00 in the evening. But not now, he couldn't decide what or how to do things. He no longer would see things to do. If I would write things down, he could do easy stuff. Cooking was now much too difficult.

A New Beginning

It was now August 2013, George was once again done with the Courage Center. Physically he was as far he could go. We talked about what happens now. Would he have to go back in from time to time for a tune up? Are we done with the neurologist? After all, what did we know? No one has ever told us what a life in a wheelchair is about. The deeper we got into this, I realized that the "what is next" for our future was that I didn't know what is in store for us. Would he stay the same? In time, would he worse, or could he get better?

I was so scared and confused. I knew I had to help him be as independent as possible. *What if something happens to me? He is so dependent on me. Especially now that his "Linda Griffiths" are gone.*

As this new life was now upon us, we were having to start dealing with work comp coming to an end. George's benefits were coming to an end. Now what for income?

George had gotten to the point where he said, "Done. No more with trying to make my broken body work *normal* again." He had come to the point where he couldn't get his hopes up only to be disappointed when nothing would change anymore.

He knew he was as far as he could go. He had to make peace with it. Was it what he wanted? No, of course not, but this was now George, take him or leave him. This is now the new *normal* George. Through all of this, I, too, have changed. It has been a heartbreaking experience with many new challenges.

Sometimes I get so mad at "it," not George, but "it." I hate "it," and "it" just happens to live in George. "IT," take a look at what you've done to our family.

Summer of 2013

Our lives were very busy, we decided to move and at the same time, it was getting time to settle up with the work comp claim.

That summer we started talking about moving and getting closer, a one-story home that would work for George. Clearly our two-story home with narrow doorways wasn't working.

At first, I didn't want to move. I loved our home. I knew we were going to take a big hit on it. I struggled with all of it; we couldn't afford to move to take such a big hit, but George was drowning there. After much thought, I realized that I had to move for George, it wasn't about me. To make him stay in that home was just wrong. I made the decision to stop being so selfish. We need to go where it was best for George. I knew that if I was the one in the wheelchair, he would move for me. *Done. We are going to move.*

But where would we go? We knew that we wanted to be closer to my work. Over the last few years, the traffic was getting so bad that if I have to move, that is the one thing I wanted. We needed a one-story that had to be handicap accessible. Time to start doing some homework. So, we went online, trying to decide if we wanted to rent or buy.

Keep in mind, George wasn't able to help much, most of it was over his head. Nevertheless, I included him in all that I would learn. We went to visit some apartments, and we decided they weren't for us.

By now it was early October 2013. We happened to drive by a really nice-looking building in New Hope. We said let's look at it. I made an appointment for us to see it.

That Saturday, we met the manger to show us the place. There were two buildings right next to each other. We thought we were going to the nicer, newer of the two. The manager thought we were talking about the older one. The older one was a rental and kind of like assisted living. The manager said, "Just come see it," so as not to hurt her feelings, and we did. I walked in there, it smelled like a nursing home. As we looked at some of the units, it was clear it wouldn't work for George. Oh, thank God! I remember thinking to myself, *I'm doing this for George, but please don't make me live in a place like that.*

After talking to the manager for a few minutes, we asked if the other building had any openings. She said yes, but it was a senior 55 plus condos not rental. We looked at each other, and said, "What do we have to lose?" After all, looking doesn't costed money, right?

We walked in, and we both looked at each other. *Oh, my God, this is it!* It was a built in 2005 but still had a lot of units for sale because of the housing market crash. We looked at the model, and we fell in love with it. Everything was perfect for George; I loved it. Now, I was a little more excited about moving. We put money down on it. Now we had to sell ours. We knew there were many units still available, and they were willing to hold it for us, no matter how long it took.

Next, we met with the developer/realtor. By mid-October 2013, our house went up for sale. We knew it might take a while as the housing market hadn't fully recovered from the crash. And yes, we were going to take a big hit on it. We knew we had to do it regardless.

Now, I had to make sure that our house looked as good as it could be 24/7. You never know when someone wants to come and see it. And the open houses were always an interruption but all part of the game. Every time there would be a showing, our hopes would go up only to be crushed when they didn't like it. That is all part of selling your home. We didn't have a lot of showings. Our realtor said it was because of the holidays. People don't want to move at this time of year. All we could do was hurry up and wait. We had a couple of people come back two to three times but in the end, they weren't the ones that bought the house.

George was getting frustrated. All of our past home sales sold before the sign went up. He couldn't understand what was taking so long. He didn't understand that the market was barley showing some signs of recovery. It was the holiday season. People were getting ready for the holidays, not house hunting.

About our fifth week in, we had a couple that found our house on the internet come to see it without a realtor. They came back three times and finally said the words we wanted to hear so badly.

"We love your house, we want to buy it!"

SOLD, the sign said! What a Christmas present!

We were so excited. We were going to be in a place that would allow George to be independent. We were scheduled to close February 14th, 2014. That was so far out, but our buyers weren't in any hurry; they hadn't even listed their house yet. We had over two months to get packed. I was dreading the packing because I knew I was going to have to do it pretty much by myself. For as many times as we have moved over the years, you'd think we'd be pros at it by now—ah, not so much.

Time to Settle Up

Not only did we have the move to deal with, but we were preparing for Arbitration settlement with work comp carrier. We would try (with the help of our attorney) to get this settled in Arbitration rather than going to court. However, if the settlement wasn't good enough, we were prepared to take it to court. I knew that would be very hard on George.

George's injuries were very serious; this was a life changing injury that left him unable to earn a living. That is how we felt the settlement should have been based on; however, work comp law had a whole other idea of what was fair. When it came down to it, it was based on his age and number of years he would work. It had nothing at all to do with the seriousness of the injury. That being said, we knew Arbitration would have to be decent. We knew we could (maybe) get a larger settlement or nothing. Still, our attorney felt we could have taken it into court and done very well.

Time for the first deposition where George would meet their attorney. This was where, for two hours, there would be questions from their attorney. George was beyond nervous and scared. He was terrified of saying the wrong thing. Their attorney was very nice, but, George was scared to death of him. You could very clearly see the fear on his face. Our attorney kept asking George if he was okay. George was scared to death but knew he had to do this if this was going to get settled. He kept telling me, "What if I say the wrong thing and screw it up for us?" All I could do is reassure him over and over again. I knew with the help of our attorney and myself, we'd had to get him through this.

We were about to start. I was allowed to sit next to George, and I held his hand so tight. Both attorneys sat across from us. The questions went well. The first part was their attorney just trying to get to know George. Then the questions began to be about the accident. This part was much harder because George didn't remember much of what happened. His processer was working very slow; it took what seemed to be forever for him to answer the questions. I wished I could have answered some of those questions for him but, all I could do was wait for him to process it and then try to answer. I was very nervous. At the same time, their attorney got to see firsthand the "new George." I remember thinking, *this is never going to end.* And then it was over.

Oh, thank goodness, it's over. One down, one to go.

I thought George did very well; he wasn't so sure. The more he would think about it, the more scared he would say over and over "what if." I told him he couldn't worry about the "what ifs" because it was over, and nothing could change it. That night, I had to reassure him over and over again. He had been so stressed that his words were very mixed up, along with not remembering. He would ask the same questions over and over again. I felt so bad for George; he was so scared that he had said the wrong thing that would mess up his settlement!

We could relax for a bit, the next (and hopefully the last one) arbitration was two weeks away.

We spent the next two weeks packing like crazy. I'm not sure why; we still weren't moving for another six to eight weeks. I think it was something to take our mind off what was ahead of us.

The closer we got to the arbitration, the more scared George was getting. His fear was growing and growing. Words and thoughts were very mixed up. The processor was very slow. He was having such a hard time comprehending things, especially when we would be talking about what was ahead. He was so scared. I knew he was counting on me to guide him through this.

It was all that was on our minds. We talked and talked. Packing seemed to be a time to hash over what we would do if they low balled us. *What would be the line for us?* At what point would we say, "Enough of this, take it into court." We knew taking it into court could maybe chances were very much in our favor but also knowing that the judge could throw it out all together, and we would lose it all. There is no going back in court. So, we had to decide to take the chance for much more money—maybe?

We had a lot to talk about; as a result, we got a lot of packing down. We were well ahead of where we needed to be for our move.

The day is here. Arbitration was at 1:00 PM in St. Paul. It was a very gloomy day. It was a very long drive for me. I was not familiar with St. Paul. George was doing his best to help me, but he was very consumed with what was ahead of him.

We were early just to be safe. I don't know that part of town or where to park. I think I was beginning to be as nervous as George, if that was possible. We sat in the lobby of this attorney's office nervously waiting, making small talk with the worker bees. Just then our attorney came in, a friendly face at last or at least someone we know.

He took us into the biggest office we had ever seen and on the 17th floor. The view was amazing, even on a cloudy rainy day.

Right away our attorney knew that something was wrong with George; his face said it all. My poor husband was scared to death, so much so I thought he was going to be sick. But, more than that, was he capable of making the decisions he would need to? Our attorney asked him many unimportant questions to see if his cognitive ability was there. At one point, our attorney looked at me and said, "I'm not sure he can do this. We may have to cancel today and get the courts to give me power of attorney."

Oh, God, I don't want that!

I knew George couldn't go through this again. Both of us just wanted it to be over.

Our attorney left us alone for a bit to talk it over. George told me he couldn't do this again and asked if I would please help him in any way I could. I told him to just breathe. The look on his face was of such fear, I just wanted to cry for him. I knew I had to be stronger than I had ever been before.

"Okay, Cathy, here we go. I took my own breath."

I looked at George and said, "Let's do this."

I gave George a big hug. I wiped the tears away from both of us.

I said, "Look at me when you get scared."

For the whole time, he looked at me. He knew I was going to get us through this.

Our attorney came back, in looked at George, and said, "Well…"

George said, "Let's do this. I CAN do this."

He still looked scared to death, but that was okay.

In our office was some high-powered attorney that our attorney knew very well. So, that was a comfort to us. We never did see the attorney or the adjuster from the work comp company.

Let's Kick Some Butt

Or, so we thought. In our office, we discussed with our attorney what to expect, how the process would go. He said the first offer would be low as our first offer would be high. That's how it worked.

The first offer was so low, I couldn't believe it. At that moment, I thought this might have to go into court. As much as I didn't think George could make it through going to court, he deserved to get the most possible. He had been through so much and will continue to for the rest of his life.

We looked at each other. Our eyes knew what we had to do. George and I have always been a team, we think very much alike. All we have to do is let our eyes talk for us.

Our time to offer; of course, as much as they low balled us, we went to the very high side. Of course, they rejected it, which we knew (but we could hope we would get them at a weak moment, and they would say yes).

We continued to go back and forth for another couple of hours. They came up, we came down. Until our attorney said that their offers were starting to be in smaller increments. He said that it was coming to an end. *What did we want to do?* Time to decide if we could accept the offer. *Do we want to go into court?* He had said that he was very confident that we could get a lot more in court. But at what price for George?

I asked for them to give us a minute alone. We both didn't want to go into court and run the risk of losing it all.

George said, "Please make it be over. I can't do anymore."

And with that, I said, "Okay."

Our attorney came back in, and we gave them one last offer—they pay all of our attorney fees along with their last offer. They agreed!

It's done!

I was never so glad of anything in my life! Poor George looked so tired. He was truly worn out. In the end, did we get what he deserved? No, of course not. To some degree, we knew that was never going happen. Minnesota work comp laws would prevent that. We accepted what we had fought so hard for. It was time for our lives to start moving forward.

It took a couple of weeks for all the paper work to process through the system, but our lives could now move forward.

I don't know what was ahead for us but like anything else we've had to face with, approach it head on with our heads hanging high.

Time to Move Onward,
Try to Make the Best of What's Left of Me

Christmas that year (2013) was no decorating as that stuff was packed ready for the move. But, that didn't matter. The lack of decorating didn't stop us from having a great time with family. Jaelyn brought so much joy to George. Her smile, laughter, and gentleness with her Grandpa was what made George fight so hard.

The first of the year, George went full time at Good Samaritan Ambassador.

Barb remembered the first couple of weeks he still struggled. He could not see the difference in what he was doing; George felt he made no impact to others. Barb talked him in to giving it some time. She reassured him that she would have his back. George was still very angry with life. He had to force a smile. Barb remembered staff stating that they had a hard time relating to him. He wasn't ready to take any of us in as friends.

One of the residents loved to play Cribbage. He asked George if he wanted to learn. To my surprise, George said yes. George didn't like to play cards. *But, I must remember this is the "New George." I don't know this one as well, but I am very willing to learn.* That night he came home with a full page of Cribbage notes.

Now, this would be a huge step forward if he can master it. George let someone in as his new friend. George and his new friend would play hour after hour, five days a week. He said he was having so much fun! There was a lot of kidding and plenty of teasing going on along with playing cards. In the beginning, George didn't win many games, but that didn't matter. He was learning something new but most of all, having fun!

This was a huge step forward for George. He learned something new he was remembering from day to day!

For the first time in years, George was excited about something. He was very good with residents and rehab patients. He could shine there; he knew it was safe, and they wouldn't judge him.

That being said, the staff would try to joke with George. He would get so pissed off and upset over what someone would say because he just could not figure out if the staff was joking. He still didn't know how to joke back with them or if they were serious.

Funny how he could joke with his Cribbage friend, not with others. I think he felt safe with his Cribbage friend. He let him in, he wasn't ready to let others in.

Barb would tell him that before he became upset and yelled back at the staff to come talk to her. Barb would help him understand the meaning of the statement. A light went on for George. That was a break through moment. "Old George" had a great sense of humor, and now the "new George" was learning how to joke. He was beginning to let more and more people in; he was feeling comfortable in both dishing it out and taking it too.

At first, they didn't really know what to do with him; they had never had someone like George volunteer.

This was a learning experience for both George and the Good Samaritan. To start with, he would put together new admit folders. The way it was set up didn't make sense to George. He asked if he could change it up some. After all, he had been a patient there and by changing the folders in a different order might be better. He showed them to Melissa (the admin person he was working with), and she loved it. It did make more sense. From that point forward, he has been in charge of putting admin folders together. Not only did he change their order, but he had developed a new system for putting them together. This would cut the time it takes to put them together in half.

The "old George" had some of the best work ethics I had ever seen. He would take tasks, make them better, and find a shorter way to do things. He was extremely organized. If there was a way to do something in a better, shorter way, he would do it. Anyone that was George's boss was very blessed to have George. He could work rings around anyone he worked with, even the older bosses.

Could this be a bit of "old George" surfacing?

Word had gotten out that George was willing to help in any way he could. The staff kept finding things for George to do. Every time something was given to him, he figured out a way to do them faster and more efficient. He was really liking all the attention he was getting. For the first time in a very long time, he was feeling good about himself and very much enjoyed what he was doing. Yes, cognitively he was starting to grow. Sometimes it would take a while to figure the task out. They were so grateful for his help and willing to help him learn.

It was the fall of 2013 that Marie (nursing home administer) came to me. She said they love having George help them, and they were so blessed to have him. I told her we were so blessed that they let George come down there and help. It had become a "win-win" for everyone. She told me that they were in the process of making up a position just for George.

He would be in charge of greeting all the new admits. He would visit them a few times while they were there. George was so excited and at the same time, terrified. Could he do it? The new George was terrified of so much.

At first, he would get so upset because he would go in the patients' rooms, and they would respond by telling him that he was in the wrong room. He would become very upset because they thought he was confused and in the wrong room because of the wheel chair.

Barb would sit with him. She asked him, "If you were in the room and somebody like George entered the room, would you be accepting? Would you not think the same thing?"

He thought about it and then the light came on. He now understood and could relax.

They both worked on a different way to introduce himself.

This took a team effort to get George to take this task on. He and I spent lots of hours going over and over the same things. As the years have gone since his injury, I have learned that if George is upset or scared, he will repeat things over and over. He will also ask the same question over and over.

Marie said that George was at his best when meeting transitional care patients. He was very welcoming and had a way about putting patients at ease through his personal experience. The patients gained a new friend and so did George. We knew that this "greeting program" would take some time to develop. That was fine, George could focus on getting packed, and Christmas was coming.

Packing seemed endless. Downsizing was hard as much as we were both throwers. *What do you do with all of this junk?* The easy part was deciding what goes and what stays. Goodwill took a lot of it, but what do you do with the stuff they don't want? The donation centers are mighty picky about what they will take. The furniture we gave to friends and family.

Closing day was getting very close; the closer it got, the less ready we seemed to be. I don't get it, we are very organized people.

I guess I was so tired I just couldn't keep doing this by myself. George would sit with me, but I needed to keep me going. Time was running out.

January 30th, 2014

It was so cold and with both doors open, the furnace didn't do much good.

The temperature was right around 0 that day.

Moving day was here. Guess what? We weren't ready. We would have to make the best of it; there was no more time to pack.

Our closings were in the morning, the movers came at 2:00 PM. We were still packing as they were moving stuff out. It took the movers a few hours to fill the truck. It was time to go to the new house. I was very excited! We would never sleep in that house of bad memories again. Goodbye, house!

The movers got finished about 8:00 PM. I was so tired, all I wanted to do was go to bed, but we had to make it up first. Ashley had gone to get some sort of fast food. Ashley and Jaelyn slept in the living room that night.

George and I talked awhile, his excitement had gone. He was terrified; this wasn't his home. We finally fell asleep, but we were both up and down that night. He was so scared. He was very glad that I was there to hold him, but all he really wanted to do was go home.

Day one in our new home was crazy, and I was so tired. I knew I had to keep going. Rose and Duane (George's sister and brother-in-law) brought hot, good food.

Rose told me to sit, that she and Ashley would unpack the kitchen. I didn't care where they put stuff. I was just so, so grateful that they would do that for me. As the boxes were emptied, Duane took them down to the recycling. By the end of the day, it was looking like there was an end to the boxes.

The first night alone in our new house, George continued to have a hard time adjusting. As much as he wanted it and needed it, it would take some time for him to get used to it before he could call it home. Cody was also having a hard time adjusting. Monday morning came, and George decided he would take the week off to help Cody settle in. The next week, I was off.

That week that George was home, he was able to unpack many boxes. He couldn't always get them put away, but he at least was able to get them in right rooms. I could then finish when I got home.

That week went fast. It was now time for George to get back to his work at the nursing home.

My New Greeting Job

Everyone welcomed him back. They were excited to see him. He, too, was excited to see all of them; after all, this was home to George.

The staff at the nursing home had begun to see how good George was with the patients. George was tired of playing cards all day with the patients. He asked Barb if there was something more he could do to help.

In all of this, he was learning again how to interact with people. And to not be so afraid of people.

Barb found that the new admin and exit folders were low. She asked if George would mind doing them; he jumped at the chance. Barb told him to make a bunch, so they would last awhile. No one liked doing them, and George didn't mind; he had made a challenge for himself. He made all the copies he would need (that took the most time). He laid the pages out in the order that he wanted them to go. He began his new task and challenge. This was very repetitive; that was how George would now learn how to do things.

A couple of hours later, he came back to Barb, he asked her where would she like them.

"What?" she said. "You aren't done, are you?"

He said, "Well, I sure am."

He had made 100 folders in a matter of a few hours.

George was very organized. He will always find a way to do something better and faster. When given a task, he will find the fastest and best way to get the job done. As we found out, that skill is still there. Once again, a little of my "old George" came out.

I wonder if this will keep happening. Time will tell!

That night when I picked him up, he had a smile on his face that told the whole story. Time to get the "greeting" program started. This was a program developed just for George. This concept of having a greeter go in and visit new patients had never been done before. George would get a list every day of new admins. He would visit them, talk with them. He had his list of questions he was to ask. He and Barb sat down and came up with a plan of attack (so to speak). He would visit with the new patients a couple of times during their stay. Some just like the visit, and some just need to be reassured that there is life after illness; after all, George was learning that very thing himself. Some would ask if they could ask how George landed in the wheelchair. It gave them something to think about; that yes, there is life after a horrific injury. The patients loved having George come visit, many of them said it made their day. It was those people who made his day, too.

At first, George was very nervous; he wasn't sure he could do this. Barb went in with him the first few visits. He went down the list of questions one by one, he got them all answered. He was pretty proud of himself and rightfully so! He did it!

The first few weeks were hard for him. Not only did he meet with all the new admins, but there was a lot of paperwork George would have to fill out for each patient he would visit with.

The hard part was keeping George on track, that was not always an easy job. If he didn't do the paperwork right away, he would forget what the visit was about. It would take a while to get his plan of attack organized and running smoothly.

Each time George would visit a new patient, it got easier and less scary. He was developing a system that worked for him. This was a very big step for George; he was learning how to interact with people and not be so afraid of people.

This was such a win-win for both George and the Good Samaritan. They were getting such good feedback from the patients; they loved him. At the same time, he was learning and growing. The best part of it all was learning to interact again.

Continuing to Grow

The summer of 2014, George was asked to join the Advisory Board. He was so excited that they thought enough of him to ask him! Then he was asked to join the spaghetti dinner committee (This was a very important committee as this was the biggest fund raiser of the year).

George and Barb talked about both of these committees; he expressed his fears. Could he do it without anyone knowing what he struggles with every day of his life?

As much as George loved going to work every day, many nights he would come home, eat dinner, and fall asleep by 7:00 PM. It takes a tremendous amount of energy for someone with a TBI to function. In some way, it's like trying to appear *normal* so people don't notice that George is different. Yes, when you first look at George, it's obvious he is different with the chair, but he works very hard not to act *stupid*—that is a big fear for him. That is the part that takes so much energy. It takes a tremendous amount of energy to act *normal* when inside you're not *normal*.

When George was at home with me, he could relax. He knew I would never judge him. I knew what his every day struggles are.

George is growing leaps and bounds, or so it seemed on the outside, but one of the things he continues to struggle with is his perception of how words don't always mean the same for him. This is still a huge struggle for him. Put his extreme sensitivity of people and his interpretation of what is being said about him or to him. His struggles are very real. You can teach him something one day; the next, he may or may not remember it. His short-term memory doesn't work very well.

Barb would contact me if there was an issue. This way we would figure out how to handle the issue. She was always been there for George and will always be there. He knew if there was a problem with someone (there are many of them) that he could talk to her and together, they would work it out. Sometimes he would need a few days at home. Barb would always let me know about the issue, so I could prepare myself of what was to come. He would be so upset and hurt. How do you tell someone that his interpretation is wrong, that they meant something entirely different? In his mind, he heard what he heard.

George was also learning how to work with caddy women that have nothing better to do than gossip. He had said many times that he would rather work with a bunch of guys any day. Everything about guys was on their shirtsleeves.

Fall of 2014

He had several advisory board meetings. He was loving it and doing very well. He knew he needed to write things down if he had any chance of remembering it. Sometimes that didn't work; the system wasn't fool proof.

They asked him to lead one of the meetings, which meant that he was in charge of keeping the meetings under control, not to let them get off track. *How funny is it that George couldn't keep himself on track, much less anyone else.* He also would lead them in prayer.

September of 2014

The nursing home had a getting fit festival. The mayor of New Hope was there along with the fitness person from the local TV station. People from the National Campus were also there. The residents and staff walked the parking lot.

Somehow the event turned to George; the people from the National Campus had heard so much about George, they were very excited to meet him. Everyone was asking to hear George's story. George would tell them all, they were just amazed how far George had come. Many of these people didn't know George's story, they just knew he was in a wheelchair.

The thing about a TBI, it is a hidden disability. If you talk to George, you may think he is just in a wheelchair but fine. Unless you really know George, you wouldn't know his daily struggles.

We didn't know at the time, but this wouldn't be the last time people wanted to hear his story.

The spaghetti dinner committee was very busy selling tickets and getting ready for their big night. George was very involved in this. He sold more tickets than anyone that year. Most of what he sold was to staff and people in the building. It didn't really matter. That fear of people was sometimes getting better. By now this was such a safe place for George.

Barb asked George if he wanted to do the computer entry that was needed to keep the ticket sales straight. He said he didn't know anything about their computer. Barb could tell that made him very nervous. Barb said that it was no problem. She would do the computer entry. He was beginning to trust Barb. Once in a while she would ask George if he wanted to try something new. In the beginning, he was much too afraid to say, "I will try that."

The night of the dinner was here, this was George's first spaghetti dinner; he was excited to be a part of it. He was collecting tickets. I got there about 5:15 PM. I watched him for a bit before he knew I was there. I was so proud of him to watch him shine. It brought tears to my eyes. He was having a great time smiling and laughing with the people. I do believe for a short period he actually forgot all he had been through. I don't know which George was there, but it didn't really matter. He was having fun and felt important.

That night I got to meet all the people he talked about so much. I got to finally put a face with a name. As I'm sure, they had heard plenty about me. I now understood about his work home. It was such a safe place for George

The win-win was really showing that night just how far George had come. They needed him, and he needed them.

When I look back, I see just how far George has really come. From right after his accident, where his cognitive ability was very low. His extreme fear of people. At the first round of therapies, the conclusion was that he would never be able to do more that stuff envelopes or be a greater at Walmart. And those first couple of years when he kept getting worse and worse. To now, October of 2014, he can smile, again talk to people, and follow commands— sometimes that is still a work in progress.

Holidays 2014

The holidays are upon us. It was our first holiday at our new home. Can you believe it has almost been one year in our new home?

It was going to be just the two of us for Thanksgiving. I made a Thanksgiving meal that was very good. We enjoyed the peacefulness of the day.

Next day, it was time to decorate for Christmas. New house, new places to put our Santas. I love to decorate the house with all our Santas. George has always enjoyed watching me find a place for them. *Hmm, where to put them?* We had a great time doing the decorating. Every Santa found a new place.

This was going to be the first Christmas in two years where we could decorate and enjoy them.

This year, George was able to help me shop for Christmas. He was so excited to shop for our now seven-year-old granddaughter. He didn't care if anyone else got anything; he was concerned about his "Little Bug." She was Grandpa's girl! We all had so much fun watching everyone open presents. Of course, when the presents were all opened, Grandpa and Jaelyn could play with all of her new games. They played for a good couple of hours. Of course, many of the games were played by Jaelyn's rules, but that didn't matter. Everyone was laughing and having a good time. To watch George interact with his "Little Bug" was the best present I could have ever gotten.

What was to Come in 2015

January of 2015

George was now volunteering 40 plus hours a week at The Good Samaritan. He was working more hours a week than most of the staff.

It didn't really matter that George was doing this work for no pay. What really mattered was how far George had come. I wondered how much further he could go. I guess time would tell.

June 2015

Barb asked George if he would like to be involved in the taco salad fund raiser. This was a small fund raiser for employees that have come into hard times. The employee assistant program. George wasn't sure he could do that. So, for the first one, he sat and watched Barb.

The next month, Barb asked him again. This time he helped dishing out the taco meat. He was doing great and was having fun. When all of a sudden, somebody didn't like how much George had given him. The guy said that George had given him less than the guy before him. George became very defensive. The guy was carrying on and on. Barb finally asked the guy to leave.

George was so upset! George had to get away. He spent the entire afternoon outside, waiting for me to pick him up. He said he was never going back! I had heard that before. We talked about it a lot that night. He stayed away for a few days. He needed some space from there. When he did go back, Barb and he talked for a very long time. He was much calmer by then. George considered the source and could now see how petty that was but still very hurtful. His feelings get hurt very easily.

His greeting program was going great. Everyone knew George, and he loved to visit with them. If George would see someone in the hall, he would stop and chat with them, asking how their day was going. Some would ask how he landed in the chair. He didn't mind sharing that with them. He still to this day doesn't remember the actual fall, but he remembers what we told him about the accident.

The feedback from the patients was great! They all loved when he would come to visit. They all said how kind, carrying, and concerned he was. He was always so encouraging. After all, he knew firsthand what it was like to come back and how important it was to have good family and friends (and grandchildren) helping.

Realty Check

Interacting with staff remained difficult for him. He would always stop to chat with most of the staff. But in doing so, it made him vulnerable. He would begin to trust them. Then someone would say something that he would interpret differently than how others would interpret it and boom, down he would come. He would be so upset. He would come home very upset. Sometimes we would talk about it over and over but what he needed to try and make sense of it.

It was very difficult for me. How can you tell someone that what he heard was not what was said? Barb would always go to the people that hurt George to get their side of story. Many of them would change their story, figuring that George didn't remember it anyway. But George did remember. He always says that he wasn't a complete idiot.

Sometimes he would take time off before he would go back. He needed time to process it. When he would go back, he was convinced that everyone was looking at him with an attitude. How do you tell someone that they are wrong, that most people don't even know what went on or even care? You can't or at least, I couldn't do that to him. It would crush him. We continued to work on his sensitivity and perception. He and Barb would talk and try to figure it out. Her hopes were that he could figure it out and how to handle it better next time.

Some of the issues came from working with women. He just couldn't understand some of the mean things they would say about each other.

I was showing George what a selfie is. So, he tried it we had a good laugh over that.

Time to Show Off

Spring 2015

George continued to shine. He was doing so many things to make a difference and at the same time, made him feel important.

He does so many things now, most of them on his own. All of the things he has mastered. Again, he develops his system and goes for it.

One day he went to Barb needing something to do.

She said, "Let me check with other the departments, and I will get back to you."

She talked to Trish (who is in charge of the clerical, medical records). She had plenty for him to do. But would he be able to do it, or would he be too scared? They decided to take it slow; she and Barb would work with him. He had seen Trish around but had never done any work for her. As he got into it a bit, he found it really easy to work with Trish.

Trish showed him how to scan medical records in to the computer. There wasn't much to it. They were so backed up, boxes and boxes that needed to be scanned into the computer. She told George to take his time, don't worry about getting this done fast. After all, they were about eighteen months behind.

George took notes, so he didn't have to bother Trish (He was never a bother).

She showed him step-by-step what needed to be done, set him up with the computer; again, she told him to take his time, no rush on this.

There were so many boxes that she figured that would keep him busy for a very long time. He could only do this part time because of all the other jobs he needed to do.

To start with, he was doing them the way she showed him, but he (as always) figured out another way to make it go faster and still do the job they way Trish needed it to be done.

He did box after box. They were all amazed at how fast this was getting done. They thought it would take him a lot longer than it did. He got them all caught up in about three months. Amazing how far he had come. I am so proud of him.

Again, he was looking for more work to do.

One day out of the clear blue, he got a phone call from Natural Campus.

Barb said, "You have a phone call?"

He couldn't figure out who would call him.

It was the national campus production office. He said they have heard so much about him and all the good things he had done. They wanted to make a film about him.

There was a story to be told, is what they said. He could not believe what he was hearing. He and Barb talked; he was so excited! Why him? The answers, why not him? After all, look at him from where he was to where he is now. What a comeback kid story.

That night, we talked about it. I was so proud of him. He has worked so hard to get to where he was. He truly had found a purpose in life.

The next few weeks were an exciting time for George. He just shined and rightfully so! After all, there should be some excitement to come out of this horrible accident.

The night before, he was very nervous. He wasn't sure he could do this. His process of slowed words were very mixed up. That "new George" was reminding us that he was still here. What if he would say the wrong thing? I told him not to be scared, that it would be alright. Barb would be there to help him. Lonnie also knew a little bit about George.

He was filming all day. The film was perfect! On March 16th, 2015, the film went viral and has been seen 424 times. I know it's not a lot of hits, but it is a small video that is designed for Good Samaritan's website: https://www.good-sam.com/locations/ambassador

Couple of weeks later, I got a call from Lonnie. It was my turn to tell the story from a caretaker perspective. The film was a success!

It made me think how much my life had really changed. It was okay to say I sometimes hate it. And how much I miss the "old George." It still is and will always be a challenge every day.

August 2015

Barb told George to come help her with something out in the parking lot. He was confused but went anyway. Outside there was a lot of co-workers. Marie gave George the surprise of a lifetime. Jackie had nominated George for volunteer of the year for the Minnesota Statewide Activity professionals. Maire told him he had been chosen out of hundreds throughout the State of Minnesota. It was the highest award a volunteer could receive.

That night he was beyond excited. I was extremely proud of him. We both cried; this time they were happy tears. He was so honored! And very humbled by this.

George is accepting his first award. To my surprise he looked at me and said he couldn't have done this without me.

The award was to be given during their convention dinner. The dinner wasn't until October 2015 up in St. Could Minnesota about Sixty miles from our house. (I sure hope our late fall weather would hold up).

WOW! Not much time to get new duds. We are jeans people, but this was a suit and tie event. It didn't take us long to find just the right outfits.

George was so excited, he couldn't wait for that night.

A couple of weeks later, he got called into Marie's office. Right away his thoughts were what did I do? Am I in trouble?

Again, her office was filled with co-workers. Marie informed him that he had been chosen for another award this time; it was from Minnesota Care Providers for outstanding service as a volunteer for 2015. This was another highest award given. This was going to be given as a part of the opening ceremony at the convention on November 16th, 2015. This, too, was unbelievable!

Good thing the grownup clothes shopping was going well, but now we had to have two different outfits. Can't wear the same thing for both awards.

George was on cloud nine and rightly so; he had worked so hard to get here. His life finally had a purpose and meaning. He felt important, needed, people value him as an important part of what makes Good Samaritan so successful.

He knows and sees that, but there are still the down times. Perception is still a problem but working very hard on that. He has gotten to the point that if it sounds different, he knows something isn't right, then he goes to Barb or me to help him work through it.

Although I can say the exact same thing to help him, and it doesn't help. If Barb says it, he gets it. When I ask him why he gets it when Barb says it but not me, he doesn't know. He is very close to Barb; she gets him and has told him she will always have his back.

I don't totally understand their relationship, but I understand he is growing and thriving because of her help. He tells me that their friendship is nothing more than a very close friendship. They count on each other.

There are times when I get jealous of her. In the beginning of this journey, he was very dependent on me for so much. That was my job to help him take care of him. He has grown to where he doesn't need me as much, but he will always need someone to help guide him, pick him up when he falls. I'm very grateful that he has Barb.

Because it was on a work night so far from home, Jackie was the only one who came from the nursing home. Jaelyn and Ashley came. Jaelyn was so proud of Grandpa. She wouldn't miss it for anything.

George was just glowing; you could see the happiness in his eyes. Lots of people came up and shook his hand, thanking him for what he does. People who didn't even know George but had heard his story said what an honor it was to meet him. George was the star of the show that night. He deserved every bit of it!

There were hundreds of people there from all over Minnesota; the president of the convention told us it could get loud during the awards. I thought that it might be a problem; George doesn't do well with lots of noise and commotion, but he handled it very well. Maybe because he was the star—who knows. He really was enjoying himself.

Time for the awards. He would be the last one to get his award (Saving the best for last). As he came to the stage, the president was telling his story. I couldn't hold back; all I could do was cry tears of joy! As he was presented the award for "outstanding volunteer of the year," everyone was clapping, all were standing. It was unbelievable! This went on for about ten minutes. He was handed the microphone as he was wiping the tears away and much to my surprise, he dedicated his success to me.

"Without the love and support from my wife, I would not be where I am today."

He also dedicated his success to Jaelyn for without all the memory games he, again, wouldn't be where he is today. People laughed at that and at the same time, were amazed that at a little five-year-old could be so important in his recovery, but she was! I couldn't stop crying; I have never been so proud of him.

That is very humbling for me; for the first time, I realized just how important I was to him. I did it because that is what you do. "In sickness and health." All along I knew if it was me in that chair, he would do the same for me. We are a team and take care of one another.

Jaelyn is at Grandpa's first award—it was very important for her to see her Grandpa get this award.

He was very humbled to win this award. It meant the world to him. Words can't even begin to describe how he was feeling, but to see the smile on his face said it all.

I remember thinking that we could now do this. This awful thing that changed our lives, so completely turned our world upside down. That now George with continued encouragement, love from his family and friends, will survive and is making a difference in this world.

I didn't want it to end! To watch him shine was amazing! Once again, people he didn't even know were coming up to congratulate him. They all wanted to know more about him. He defiantly was the star of the dinner.

The drive home was filled with excitement from what had just happened. Going to bed that night wasn't easy; we just hugged each other, talking about the dinner. We talked for a long time before we fell asleep.

The next day at work, everyone wanted to hear all about it. It turned out that the next day, he, again, was the star.

Now it was time to get back to work; the second award was a few weeks away yet. George and Barb continued to work on the greeting program. It had been a huge success. They followed up with thank-you cards. Quite often they will be returned with compliments about George and what a wonderful, helpful man he is to both the patient and family members.

This program has been refined and defined along the way. Barb and George meet when they get time to go over what is working and what is not. They are finding that some people respond to George better than Barb. Or the other way around. Some just respond better to one or the other for whatever reason. Sometimes they have to be flexible enough. The last thing they want is to upset the patient.

As time has gone on, Barb has taught George how to do many of the things she does. At first, he is real scared, but she will write up directions of what to say on the phone calls, his cheat sheets. Before you know it, he is making the phone calls all by himself without out cheat sheets.

They find when he mails out innovations for the rehab brunch, he will make follow-up phone calls. As a result, the turnout has been great! They are getting more people than ever. George has become very good on the phone. He likes talking to these people.

November is rolling around, fall is in the air.

George & I at his first award I was SO proud of him.

November 16, 2015

It is a cold, rainy, misty day. The day has come for George's second award. We were not as nervous for this one. After all, it was just four weeks earlier when he got his first award.

This was an afternoon event and in Edina, MN, so many more family and friends were able to come.

Linda Griffith had called a few days earlier, she said had some serious health issues she was dealing with and wouldn't be able to come. That saddened George. He had planned on dictating this award to her. Because without all the patients, kindness, and encouragement, he wouldn't be where he is today. She gave him the tools, and he ran with it.

We knew his two sisters and their husbands, Ashley and many of his friends/co-workers from The Good Samaritan would be there. He had so many friends, family, and co-workers that we took up the first two rows. I think at that moment, George realized just what a huge support system he really had.

George on stage accepting is second award

There were at least three to five hundred people there. They came from all over the state for this convention. George's award was to be given as the opening of the convention.

The president of Minnesota Care Providers began telling George's story, going into some detail. As he is talking about his story, Jackie began to roll him to the ramp. People were standing and clapping and cheering for him. Again, the tears began to roll and again, they are happy tears. As he was center stage, the light shined on him and rightfully so. It took a lot of blood, sweat, and tears for George to be where he is at that moment.

Ashley, George & Jaelyn after the first award

The cheering went on for at least fifteen minutes. His speech was a general one, thanking all who have helped him to get where is today. He said he was so honored to accept this award! And he will continue to do the work he loves so much.

There were flashes everywhere, and everyone wanted a picture of George. Everyone wanted to talk to him. They wanted to hear more about his story and the courage it took to get here.

It took us about 45 minutes to get out of there. He had become overwhelmed. We finally got to our car, and I asked George if he wanted to go out to eat and celebrate. He said he was so tired, he just wanted to go home. So, that is what we did.

George was so worn out, he slept for hours. Rest was what he needed. I knew it had been too much for him as his words were mixed up. He was processing very slowly.

He wasn't done with his "fame," but it was beginning to be too much. The next day, property manager from our condo asked if she could interview George; she wanted to put an article in our little monthly newspaper. Everyone heard about George. He was done. He couldn't do it anymore. I told her, "Not now. He is just too worn out and overwhelmed." She understood.

Back at work, George began showing stress signs. He was very overwhelmed. He was talking to Barb more and more. She was his go-to person. He would come home crabby, falling asleep right after dinner. At first, I didn't know what was wrong. Barb, Jackie, and I were in close contact, trying different things that might bring George back to where he was before all of the attention of his co-workers. They were coming to Barb and me, asking, "What is wrong with George?" He was snapping at people; his struggles were very apparent. This time, everything was on his shirt sleeve. You never knew if he was sad or angry, but if you tried to talk to him, you would know. His co-workers gave him the space he needed.

It took months for George come around. We took it one day at a time. Some days were better than others. What we discovered was his world needs to be simple with pretty much the same routine every day. He needed to start using the skills that Linda Griffin gave him.

So, back to the planner and few other goodies that helped a lot. He had to learn to say "no," that he didn't have time rather than "yes" to everyone. For a while, all work requests went through Jackie. This helped with being so overwhelmed. When he wasn't so overwhelmed, he was more at peace with himself.

George has now been at The Good Samaritan for four years. He is thriving in his new life. He has his struggles, each day brings new challenges for him, sometimes he can handle them and some days not so much, but he has the knowledge, skills to get up dust off his pants, and go on. He is finally at peace with himself, and he is happy!

Epilogue

As I get closer to getting this book published; I want to share some updates since the end of the book.

George continues to volunteer full time at Good Samaritan he loves it. He feels good about himself when he is helping others. He and Barb have become very good friends. George is wanting to learn every thing he can. Barb is very willing and patient with George. He says she knows to go slow with him he is not afraid when she is teaching him something new.

He continues to struggle with perception issues. When George's feelings get hurt from a perception issue he will go to Barb to talk through it. Sometimes he will just take a break from the nursing home. He is beginning to see when his perception is different from others or how it was really meant. That is a work in progress and may always be trouble for George.

George continues to grow both mentally & physically in the last few months he's got a very good report from his eye Dr. His Optic nerve has healed improving his vision. After his accident we were told that his vision would never improve.

He really isn't in any pain—for the most part he is pain free. If you recall we were told he would be a great deal of pain the rest of his life.

Most recently: He does a lot of scanning and Indexing at Good Samaritan as a volunteer. Over the years a part time scanning (paid position) position would be available; every time this position was open George would talk about applying, but never could get the courage to apply. Well, this time the position again became available; he talked to Barb and I about applying. He was again nervous and somewhat afraid he decided on his own to apply for the part time scanning and indexing position. As the application process moved along he again was nervous; he talk about why he couldn't do the job, but didn't back out, one interview after another (Barb and I would keep encouraging him).

Well I'm very proud to say that George got the Job! He is now an employed, another thing they said he would never be able to do.

He is ready for it and he can do it!

As we are coming close to the seven-year mark—the day that changed our lives forever. George continues to grow and beat the odds. He is doing things that we were told he would never be able to do again.

He is determined to regain some of what was taken from him.

Sky is the limit for him!

Catherine Rosch

*Tools to Start a Daily Practice
and Stick With It!*

Meditation

for Transformation

Journal

Rebekah Joy Luhrs

Night Hawk Publishing

Contents

Praise for M4T Journal

"Written with simplicity and Rebekah's quiet, compassionate authority, *Meditation for Transformation Journal: Tools to start a daily practice and stick with it!* is the best resource I have read for helping humans develop and sustain a meditation habit. Offering practical ways to design and sustain your meditation practice, it is easy to read and to be enchanted by."

- Kimberly Hughes, M.S.Ed., CHt, CRS, Sacred Self Living

"The story drew me right in from the beginning... Very inviting for people to discover themselves and make this their own personal practice." This is the perfect meditation guide, not too much, not too little. Rebekah seamlessly integrates personal story, wisdom teaching, and practical application to help anyone deepen their meditation practice.

- Mackenzie McDonald Wilkins, Asheville Area yogi, energy body worker, herbalist, musician, dancer, nature lover, and space holder

This journal is multi-tooled providing a deep dive into inner knowing and keeping my practical life on track! The habit tracker was essential in bringing to life the insights I received through meditation."

- Alexis Dias, Author of *Our Sunty*

Dedication

To the Communities of Western North Carolina—

In the wake of Hurricane Helene, you became the light in the darkness, meeting devastation with a kind of resilience that defies explanation. The way you showed up for one another - with grit, generosity, and a fierce tenderness - has set in motion a new path for how we will be in community, how we will rebuild sustainably, and how we will live in tune with nature's wisdom.

To my community in and around Asheville, NC—

Thank you for your steady support of my personal journey, and for the raw enthusiasm (and patience!) you've offered as this journal came to life.

To **Kim Hughes**—your advocacy for those willing to rewrite their inner narratives and live into their full potential has been a guiding light. You inspire me to keep showing up.

To **Mackenzie McDonald Wilkins**, **Adrien Calloway**, and **Alysha Beckner**—your intimate reflections, honest feedback, and encouragement helped shape this journal.

To **Salina Hernandez**—your devotion to refining this project and your tireless commitment (editing *twice!*) establishes a powerful clarity.

To **Amadell**—for the land and chosen family who held me through a time of deep creativity and growth—thank you. This journal is rooted in your love.

And to **OM Sanctuary,** *especially Shelli Standback*—Thank you for trusting me, welcoming me, and holding space for creative healing during a time of chaos and deep uncertainty. Without the refuge you offered, this publication would not have been possible. This journal is nourished by your faith and trust.

Introduction

This journal started as an almost-dare in March 2024. "Can you write a book under 5,000 words, in three days, without researching a subject?" an instructor in a class proposed. The invitation ignited something inside me, and I wondered, *What do I know from my life experience that could benefit others?* The answer came before the question had even finished forming: Tools for starting a daily meditation practice.

A few months before the unintended dare, my partner of seven years asked for a separation. Fully committed to our journey together, I sat in shock as he spoke, seated next to me on the couch in my music room. As words poured from him, it was clear he came to this decision on his own. Behind my deer-in-the-headlights eyes, waves of shock and disbelief tore through my body like earthquakes.

"How did I not see this coming?" I wondered in disbelief. Anger and shock burned beneath my skin for believing we were weathering a marriage's natural ebb and flow. I sat bewildered as his words stripped me of our friendship, our home, and a community we spent four years cultivating. Standing on the precipice of an unwritten future, I felt raw and vulnerable, completely uprooted.

From a bird's eye view, I watched myself lean into the wind and trust. I half expected my sense of security and internal stability to unravel completely, *Who is this person?!* As I tuned into the unexpected strength and stability within, I felt the currents of my meditation practice weaving an inner foundation. While tears and grief flowed outward, the roots of my daily practice held me, like an oak standing firm in a windstorm.

The Start of a Meditation Guide

Having experienced the transformative qualities of a regular meditation practice, I knew the greatest gift I had to offer was sharing the tools that helped me create a sustainable daily practice. Two days into writing, I had triple the word count yet barely scratched the surface. Realizing this would be more than a quick guide, I transformed the challenge into something deeper: I was writing a full-length meditation book.

I spent winter and spring fully immersed in writing while living in my van. My office? The nearly empty dining room of Panera Bread in East Asheville. With their Sip Club membership, I spent guilt-free hours using their WiFi, outlets, and comfortable booths flooded with abundant sunlight. However, as summer approached, I craved more structure and stability.

A friend connected me with Oshun Mountain Sanctuary (OM Sanctuary), a holistic retreat center in Asheville, North Carolina, where I was later accepted for an artist residency beginning in early October. It was a collaborative opportunity that offered space to explore and develop my work while supporting guest programs and leading meditation sessions during weekend retreats.

Heaven and High Water

A week before my start date, I was in Crestone, Colorado, on a yearly pilgrimage to the Sangre de Cristo Mountains. After seven days of practice at 12,000 feet and studying Tibetan Life Force Yoga with my teacher Peter May, we hiked down to the news of Hurricane Helene devastating all of Western North Carolina. For days, there was no way to contact friends back home or to know if they were okay. All communications were down because flood waters and wind storms annihilated electrical systems and cell towers.

Roads and bridges leading into the city were destroyed or blocked by debris, and a section of I-40 was completely washed out. Even if I wanted to, there was no way to get home. Frozen, once again with disbelief and uncertainty, I stayed in Crestone until I received clear direction.

A week after my initial start date, I got a hold of OM Sanctuary. Perched above the French Broad River and overlooking the River Arts District, their property was safe from the raging waters. The storm winds, however, swept through their forested campus like a couple of toddlers playing with pick-up sticks.

Trees over a century old now lay interwoven across the property, blocking access to the entire campus. Oaks landed on the roofs of newly renovated cottages, poplars mangled gates, and other trees damaged multiple structures including crushing a transformer. Amazingly, everyone was safe, including the only staff member onsite working security.

In the weeks that followed, a team of volunteers and heavy machinery miraculously arrived to cut through the wall of fallen trees at OM Sanctuary. It took two weeks to unbury the campus and 13 days for power to be restored. I got the call on day 19 just two hours after the non-potable water was returned to the main building where I was to reside. When I picked up, I knew my residency would look much different.

Amid all the unknowns, OM Sanctuary's CEO, Shelli Standback, invited me to begin the residency. Trusting her instincts, she welcomed me to join the onsite efforts focused on recovery and community relief. Within days, I was driving cross-country, stopping only to collect donations and load needed supplies into my van.

Recovery and Resilience

When I got back, everyone I knew was in survival mode. Several close friends lost nearly everything while others opened their homes and shared resources. The community came together with a powerful force. Leaders emerged from the mud, organizing neighborhoods and communities. Everyone was asking, "How can I help?!" People and pets were being rescued, families fed and housed, access to basic amenities were set up, and resource centers were established. An invisible force moved through each person like a superpower: powers of compassion, selflessness, stamina, and grace. People cared for one another and lifted each other, ushering in a new understanding of the word "resilience."

Those who live through a natural disaster know that the storm is only the beginning—recovery becomes a lifestyle in the years that follow. Being spared from the direct trauma of Hurricane Helene, I came back with fresh vigor, ready to offer my support and uplift those around me. In the midst of it all, I wished I had a completed guide to share—tools to offer stability in times of upheaval.

The Birth of This Journal

As Asheville transitioned from survival mode into the daily grind of filing for insurance claims and rebuilding, I slowly returned to writing. As an artist-in-residence, people increasingly asked about my creative project. Every time I mentioned the upcoming meditation guide, faces lit up. The response was always the same:

"Oh, I need that!" "When will it be out? "Can I pre-order it?" Their enthusiasm was contagious, but instead of feeling excitement, my heart would sink. Frustration crept in. I wished I were further along. After an unexpected five month break, there was still so much work ahead.

It was time to shift gears. While large sections of the guide remained unfinished, most of the habit-forming resources and accountability tools were already outlined and developed. Wanting to offer support now, I decided to simplify the process and release what I had so far in the form of a journal, *Meditation for Transformation Journal: Tools to Start a Daily Practice and Stick With It!* By releasing the journal first, I would have a tool to share with others as I continued to develop the more in-depth guide.

My Meditation Journey

I experienced my first meditation practice unexpectedly in 2006 while studying at Yonsei University in South Korea. One day, while wandering the streets of Seoul with a friend, we stepped into a temple bookstore and met a resident Buddhist monk, Meo-Kung Sunim. He led us to the main temple and introduced us to a simple self-awareness meditation technique.

On the third floor of a temple tucked within a metropolis four times the size of New York City, I felt a stillness growing within myself. In the months ahead, I returned to the temple to practice regularly, adopting the technique as my own.

In the years that followed, my practice evolved. I immersed myself in yoga and eventually pursued a 200-hour yoga teacher training. It was here, in 2015, that I first committed to a daily meditation practice—and it shook me.

Attempting a Daily Practice

During training, we were required to meditate daily and keep a log. Until then, my meditations were inspired by sacred spaces and the gentle murmur of waterfalls—places where stillness naturally thrives. I entered feeling confident in my sporadic practice but was quickly humbled.

The first day on my mat, I faced a shocking reality: My thoughts were anything but quiet and peaceful. When I sat down, I came face to face with an angry caged animal. My mind was anything but still. I was hit with a wall of errands, phone calls, laundry, and other tasks I had to do. All surfacing at once, it took every ounce of self-control not to grab my notebook and make a list.

In week two, I noticed subtle shifts. My thoughts settled more easily into stillness, sometimes resting there for a few minutes, other times for a mere 30 seconds. In these moments, my whole being took a long, deep breath. Slowly, I let go of my need to control.

In week three, I began to notice shifts outside of my practice. I felt more at ease throughout the day. Tasks once stressful now felt less urgent. I noticed that I began to crave the stillness in my practice: the moments when mental stressors dissolved and were replaced by a simple presence.

Still, getting on my mat was a mental battle. In week three, I began to drop in and was present after a few breath exercises. The more I connected inwardly, the more my mind sat with me, like an old friend.

In week four, I felt deep clarity and spaciousness. Thoughts and ideas came out of thin air. Simple hunches like "grab an umbrella" on a day it unexpectedly poured on my walk home, or "call your sister" when she was having a rough day. After 30 days of meditating, I felt the force of the universe at my back.

Thinking I could maintain my practice by meditating just a few times a week, I did not continue the daily practice when the training ended. How wrong I was. After a few days off, my mind reverted to its busy, fluttering state, unwilling to relinquish control for even 12 minutes. A few months later, I tried to incorporate a 5-minute daily practice alongside my yoga routine. It wasn't the same, and after another few months, I gave up the battle and returned to meditating sporadically.

Feeling my best self during meditation, I haphazardly attempted to revive my daily practice. Seeking motivation, I explored numerous texts and inspirational videos. Looking for structure, I dabbled in meditation calendars and low-commitment journals. Every six months or so, I chased something new, like a fleeting fad.

In 2020, everything I needed to build and commit to a daily meditation practice finally came together. *Meditation for Transformation Journal: Tools to Start a Daily Practice and Stick With It!* is a culmination of the resources I discovered on my journey to commit to a sustainable daily practice. Outlined in a clear and concise format, it is my deepest desire that these tools support you in accessing your inner wisdom by starting a daily meditation practice.

As you explore these resources, you may find success with just a few of these tools, while others may benefit from using them all. The invitation is to take what works for you.

Onward

It has been over a year since my failed almost-dare, and I am deeply grateful for the journey. I watch in awe as my practice continues to bring clarity and grounding, serving as a steady anchor through life's storms. Whether navigating the upheaval of a hurricane or moving through a divorce, meditation offers me a place of assuredness amidst the chaos.

You, too, have access to a grounding force within, and meditation is the gateway to accessing it.

May these tools support you in showing up each day, help facilitate the inner conversation, and empower you to create the life you are worthy of.

With deep gratitude and joy,

Rebekah Joy Luhrs

March 6, 2025

Chapter 1

What is Meditation?

"There is no other spiritual teacher than your own soul."

— Swami Vivekananda

Meditation is the practice of turning inward, cultivating stillness, and becoming more present and aware of ourselves and the world around us. It has been practiced for thousands of years across many cultures and traditions, each with its unique approach, while also sharing a common essence: the exploration of awareness, inner peace, and connection. At its core, meditation is not about achieving a particular state of being but about learning to be present moment by moment. Whether seeking clarity, stress reduction, or a deeper relationship with self, meditation offers a simple yet profound path—one that is open and available to all, regardless of where each person is on their journey.

Reasons Why People Meditate

People from all walks of life and cultures around the world are drawn to meditation for a variety of reasons. Here are some common reasons:

- Focus and Awareness
- Relaxation
- Stress Reduction
- Health Benefits
- Connection to Oneness
- Introspection and Self-Inquiry

There Is No Destination

Most of us are introduced to meditation in its more refined or idealized forms: We picture the stereotypical calm-faced Buddha overlooking a sunrise or a monk sitting for long hours in a temple. Maybe we envision a guru with no worldly desires or a saint who's transcended suffering. In these instances, we inadvertently see meditation as an elevated state of being rather than as a continuous process. What we don't see is the journey it takes to get there and the growth still to come.

Expectations versus Reality

It Can Feel Like Work

Unless we are accustomed to being in stillness, our first experiences with meditation can feel anything but peaceful and quiet. In the fast-paced world we live in, we are constantly jumping from one task to the next. Being fully present with our thoughts and emotions is not something we are used to. In the first few sessions, everything buried inside of us can rise to the surface. For some, it is overwhelming, each thought and feeling demanding to be noticed. But these thoughts and emotions are not obstacles to overcome, they are the keys to our transformation. With dedication to the practice and compassion for ourselves, we start to understand the inner workings of our mind and emotions over time. Our thoughts begin to settle, and our mind starts to ease.

There Is No Fast Track

When we approach meditation with expectations of how we should feel, we try to force an outcome or fix a problem. It is common to think we should silence our thoughts or rise above them, even override or replace them with seemingly more positive thoughts. But meditation isn't about forcing change— it's about meeting each moment as it is and allowing space for what arises.

When we push away uncomfortable thoughts or emotions without first acknowledging them, they usually find their way back in. Meditation invites us to be present with what comes up, allowing our thoughts and emotions, even the ones that feel difficult, to be witnessed. When we understand why thoughts and emotions arise, we can acknowledge, release, and transform them into qualities that better serve us. The more we practice, the more we discover—not by forcing anything, but by showing up with curiosity and compassion.

Ever-Changing Practice

We are ever-changing beings, which is why each time we sit to meditate the experience is different. As we become aware of our shifting thoughts and emotions, we meet ourselves as we are. Each day brings something new—whether in our circumstances or within ourselves—making our practice different every time. The aim is simple: to meet each moment with awareness and allow it to be as it is.

The Right Way to Meditate

The only way to do it wrong is not to do it. Meditation isn't about getting it right—it's about showing up, sitting in silence, and being present with what surfaces. While there are many techniques to explore, the practice itself isn't rigid. It's not about achieving a perfect state or following a strict formula; it's about allowing yourself to be exactly where you are. Some days will feel effortless and others challenging, but every moment of stillness is precious. The "right" way to meditate is the one that feels best for you.

The Spiritual Nature of Meditation

In our physical body it is easy to lose sight of our innate connection to something greater. Some may call it God, the Great Spirit, the Creator, the Goddess, the Universe, Cosmic Consciousness, Source Energy, or even the unfolding of evolution. However we understand it, we are inseparable from the fabric of existence, with the power of creation flowing through us. By nature, we are powerful creators, and direct access to this power lies within us.

When we sit in silence and tune into our internal world, a doorway opens for us to reconnect with this essential part of us. I once heard a quote by Sadhguru saying, "Prayer is when you speak to God, meditation is when God speaks to you." As we create space for that still, small voice to be heard, meditation is an opportunity for conversation to flow both ways.

Connecting with the Field

The practices in this guide are designed to quiet the mind, creating space to connect with what lies beyond it: a field of infinite potential. In my experience, being in this field is a state of complete surrender: A stillness that exists beyond the breath, a silence that rests beyond thoughts, a space of timelessness and pure awareness where there is nothing "to do," only a gentle reminder to "be." It can feel like dissolving into nothing and expanding into everything simultaneously. In essence, it is being in union with the source of existence.

Many spiritual and mystical traditions directly recognize this idea of a field (or what it represents) as an all-pervading, intelligent, creative source beyond space and time and accessible through inner stillness, meditation, or revelation. Though the language varies, the essence is similar:

- **Brahman** - In Hinduism, it is known as the infinite, unchanging reality beyond time, space, and causation: pure consciousness and the source of all existence.
- **God Consciousness** - In spiritual and mystical traditions, they recognize an all-pervading, intelligent, creative source beyond space and time and accessible through inner stillness, meditation, or revelation.
- **The Quantum Field** - In physics, it's described as a field of energy where everything originates: particles, forces, and even matter itself are seen as ripples or movements within this invisible field. It's a space of infinite potential.
- **Space** - In Yungdrung Bön, the ancient spiritual tradition of Tibet that predates Buddhism, it is known as the primordial, formless ground of being that is described as the vast, luminous, and unchanging

source of all phenomena and the natural state of the mind.

- **The Tao** - In Taoism, it is the formless flow underlying and connecting all life, the origin of the universe and natural order, and the source of all things.
- **Universal Consciousness** - in Panpsychism / Idealism is a philosophical view that consciousness is the fundamental substance of the universe.
- **The Web of Life** - In Shamanic traditions, this field is referred to as a vast, intelligent force that animates all life and connects all beings across seen and unseen realms.

Since the early 2000s, Dr. Joe Dispenza has been instrumental in bringing the concept of the quantum field into mainstream awareness. Building on ideas from quantum physics and neuroscience, his books and workshops—especially *Breaking the Habit of Being Yourself* (2012), *You Are the Placebo* (2014), and *Becoming Supernatural* (2017)—have popularized the notion that through meditation and elevated states of emotion, individuals can access a field of infinite potential to create personal transformation and healing. In many of his talks and guided meditations, he refers to this field as the invisible realm where all possibilities exist, where matter hasn't yet collapsed into form, and where time and space don't operate the same way.

So, how do we get there?

Again, the goal of meditation is not to "get" anywhere. If you subscribe to the idea of the field, it is essentially the container of all existence. It is a constant, and we interact with it continuously in varying degrees of awareness. In meditation, when we disconnect from our learned identity and limited perceptions of reality, we more easily perceive the field. As we clear energies such as thoughts, emotions, judgments, and attachments, we can access deeper states of connection and consciousness. The practices in this guide can be stepping stones to connecting with this field.

Though connecting with this field is possible, it may or may not happen for everyone, and it surely is not the goal. The power of meditation lies in stillness and silence and in bringing our awareness to what arises without trying to control an outcome.

Meditation for Transformation Overview

The Weight of Inherited Truths

Much of what comes up in meditation is not truly ours. As social beings, we adopt identities so that we can belong. Over time, this shapes a long list of thoughts and beliefs that are not true. As children, we play fearlessly—until an adult scolds us for being too loud and teaches us shame. Many of us are told to dream big, and that anything is possible—yet we often encounter narrow definitions of success. We are told to love everyone, yet warned not to 'hang out with the wrong crowd.' We are made to feel guilty for following our hearts instead of meeting others' expectations. When we attach ourselves to a person or a role that falls apart, we experience fear and loss. We tend to carry a sense of obligation for responsibilities that were never ours to bear. Through our awareness in meditation, we begin to unravel and detach from these "truths" that are not ours.

Letting Go of Old Beliefs

Similarly, we come face to face with beliefs we hold—ones we may have carried for years: the ideas that we must prove our worth, that we don't deserve to take up space, or that we must meet others' expectations to be loved. Beliefs like these feel deeply ingrained; yet when we examine them, we see they aren't who we are.

To know ourselves fully, we must strip away the identities and beliefs that no longer feel true to us. Much of meditation is unlearning who we have been taught to be so that we can reconnect with our authentic selves and the unlimited possibilities within us.

Meditation is not about achieving stillness or getting it right; it's about showing up, again and again, with an open heart and a willingness to be present. Some days may feel effortless, others may feel heavy, but each moment you spend in silence is an opportunity to meet yourself more fully. There is no bypassing, and there are no shortcuts—only the practice of being with what is, allowing it to rise, and learning to let go of what you don't need. Over time, the noise settles, not because you force it to, but because you learn to sit with it, to listen, and to transform it. Through that transformation, you don't become someone new, you simply remember who you've been all along.

Chapter 2

How to Use This Journal

"Yesterday I was clever, so I wanted to change the world. Today I am wise, so I am changing myself."

— Rumi

H onestly, you could skip all of the chapters, go straight to the journal pages, and start meditating today! However, if you have this book in your hand, you are most likely seeking additional structure and support. With that in mind, here is what's ahead:

This Journal Offers:

- A brief overview of meditation
- An introduction to foundational meditation practices
- Transformational meditation practices

- Six weeks of daily journal pages for continued reflection

This Journal is NOT:

- A deep dive into the history of meditation
- A comprehensive overview of health and wellness benefits
- An exploration of lineages and traditions
- A scientific review of meditation research

The M4T Path

The *Meditation For Transformation Journal: Tools to start a daily practice and stick with it!* (M4T Journal) is a road map for empowering a daily meditation practice - providing structure, accountability, simplified techniques, and tools to develop and sustain a routine.

The M4T Journal invites you to:

1. Commit to a daily practice
2. Choose a path that fits your needs
3. Meditate for 15 minutes a day
4. Log your experience for six weeks (42 days)
5. Explore different meditation techniques
6. Explore accountability tools
7. Develop a personalized and sustainable practice

1. **Make the Commitment**

In Chapter 8, before you start day one, you are invited to make a formal commitment to yourself, your family, your community, and/or to a higher power to practice daily. Not to be taken lightly, this commitment reflects why a meditation practice is important to you.

2. **Choose a Path That Fits Your Needs**

Honoring individual levels and experience, *M4T Journal* offers three paths to choose from. Path One is fully guided and simplified for those who want to follow a program. Path Two is self-guided, offering modifications for those with more experience and desiring flexibility. Path Three is fully modified, inviting seasoned practitioners to make the practice their own while taking advantage of the accountability tools offered. All three paths are outlined in detail in Chapter 7, "Getting Started: Choose Your Path."

3. **Why 15 Minutes?**

Fifteen minutes offers a solid foundation for building a lasting practice. It's enough time for the nervous system to start to settle, shifting from sympathetic (fight-or-flight) to parasympathetic (rest-and-digest) mode and for the mind to move beyond surface-level distractions into a more grounded awareness. While short sessions are also beneficial, research from Judson Brewer and colleagues (2011) shows that around 12–15 minutes of meditation is when the brain begins to exhibit meaningful changes in the default mode network—an area associated with self-referential thinking and mind-wandering. For many, five or ten minutes can pass without settling into the practice, while twenty can feel daunting at the outset. Fifteen minutes provides a supportive threshold—long enough to be transformative, yet accessible enough to return to daily.

4. **Why Six Weeks?**

Many resources and motivational speakers suggest that it takes between 21 and 66 days for a new habit to stick, varying of course from person to person. With this in mind, a six-week program serves as a happy medium for developing a solid foundation. Six weeks is also equal to 42 days. For those who are familiar with Douglas Adams' *The Hitchhiker's Guide to the Galaxy* series, you know that the number 42 is presented as the answer to the

ultimate question of life, the universe, and everything. Seems like an appropriate place to start!

5. **Meditation Techniques**

With a focus on cultivating inner stillness and silence, the *Meditation for Transformation Journal* (M4T) primarily uses a blend of mindfulness meditation, breath awareness, body scan, and guided visual meditation techniques. As you develop your practice, you are highly encouraged to explore other meditation styles and incorporate them. Here are some you may have heard of, starting with those used in this guide:

- Mindfulness Meditation
- Breath Awareness
- Guided Visualization Meditation
- Body Scan
- Walking Meditation

- Loving-Kindness Meditation (Metta)
- Breath Work
- Sound Meditation
- Chakra and Energy Activation
- Mantra Meditation

6. **Accountability Tools**

Chapters 5 and 6 provide tools and resources for building a sustainable practice. You'll find strategies for external accountability—like support from friends and groups—along with practical tools such as journal pages and a habit tracker that help with internal accountability.

7. **Developing a Personal Practice**

At the end of 42 days, a process is offered to support you in developing a personalized meditation practice. With complete freedom to modify and restructure your approach, the exercises empower you to create a daily practice that aligns with your lifestyle, needs, and intentions. Use the M4T program as a foundation to build on, or start with a blank canvas!

Support Materials

Meditation Scripts

Scripts, the written-out guided meditations, are provided as a reference for self-guided meditations. For those who prefer to create their recordings, use these tips when reading aloud.

Tips for Recording Scripts:

- **Find a Quiet Place:** Avoid recording where background noise is distracting.
- **Read Slowly and Calmly**: Maintain a steady pace, taking extended pauses at commas and periods.
- **Text in Brackets:** This text is unspoken.
- **[Two full breaths]:** This is a queue to incorporate the full length of the number of breaths listed to ensure the recording is 15 minutes in length. Using gentle, audible breaths can help guide listeners and encourage continued breathing. Breaths can also be incorporated silently, depending on personal preference.

Meditation Recordings

Each recording is about 15 minutes long and uses an audible breath as a metronome to incorporate periods of silence for unguided meditation. If the audible breaths are too distracting, audio versions without these are also available in the "Supporting Resources" section.

Access to guided recordings is offered through QR codes and website links. QR codes are found at the start of Chapters 9 and 10, while web addresses are provided in the "Supporting Resources" section.

- **Audio Files:** Stored on a Google Drive, these can be downloaded to your device for use offline.
- **YouTube Videos:** As another access point, meditations can be referenced in a provided YouTube Playlist.

Writing Prompts

Occasional prompts are offered to support deeper reflection. Feel free to explore them by writing, thinking through them quietly, or skipping them—whatever feels right for you.

Habit Tracker

This monthly habit tracker helps you stay accountable by tracking up to 20 daily habits and offering a visual reminder of your intentions and progress throughout the month.

These are found in Chapter 6 under "Accountability Tools."

Journal Pages

The journal pages help you stay committed by offering daily entry templates to track sessions, note challenges, and reflect on your experience. They create a sense of daily accountability, and past entries can reveal patterns, highlight growth, and keep you motivated. Over time, the journal becomes a supportive companion, reminding you of your progress and the benefits of showing up.

These are found in Chapter 11 with detailed instructions offered in Chapter 6 under "Accountability Tools."

Further Reading

For those interested in the history and lineages of meditation, yoga philosophy and practice, the neuroscience of meditation, and more, visit the section "Further Reading."

Chapter 3

Starting Your New Routine

"Successful people are simply those with successful habits."

— Brian Tracy

Our bodies thrive on rhythm. The habits we repeat each day don't just shape how we move through the world, they quietly shape what's happening inside us, too. Things like brushing our teeth, making coffee, or driving to work often happen on autopilot because we've done them so many times; they are a part of us. These small routines might seem insignificant, but over time, they influence how we feel, how we think, and how we show up, often without us even noticing.

Each of these routines began as a conscious effort— something you had to remember, decide, and repeat. Over time, these routines became automatic. The same is possible with meditation. What starts as an intentional practice can, with consistency, become as natural a part of your day as brushing your teeth or steeping your morning tea.

Common Challenges

Starting a meditation practice is similar to developing any new habit. It requires time and commitment to build consistency and stamina. When we engage in a new physical activity, like a workout, our bodies aren't accustomed to the effort and physical strain. The first week or two may be tough, but we keep going, knowing the effort supports our well-being.

The same is true for meditation. Our bodies aren't used to stillness, and our minds aren't accustomed to silence. In the beginning, this shift can feel far from relaxing, but just as our bodies can adjust to a new physical routine, our minds can also adapt to a mental one.

Behaviors versus Habits

When we commit to a daily meditation practice, we introduce a new behavior into our routine. In the beginning, it takes a lot of effort to show up. Our bodies resist change and prefer to sleep in and revisit familiar habits. However, as we continue to practice, neural pathways in the brain that support this new behavior strengthen and become more efficient.

Research in neuroscience and psychology shows that changing habits requires focus, intention, and repetition. Over time, the new behavior becomes more natural and effortless. By staying intentional and consistent, we create the neural pathways that turn behaviors into lasting habits.

Consistency and Discipline

Similar to learning a new skill, such as playing an instrument or learning a language, meditation requires steady effort to maintain progress. For me, when it comes to consistency and discipline, meditation is a lot like rock climbing. Building the strength to climb a moderate-grade face takes months. Climbers need consistent practice to keep progressing. If I take a week off, I feel like I lose all momentum. While muscle memory remains, my strength and endurance seem to disappear overnight. After just a week off, my body can feel like I spent a month on the couch eating Five Guys!

The same is true for my meditation practice. When I miss even one practice, the busyness of my mind regains ground. When given the opportunity, old patterns creep back in, reestablishing their hold and filling in the space previously cleared. Personally, if I miss a day, it can take several more to get back to where I was. Skip longer, and it often feels like starting from scratch.

Establishing a new routine is never easy. At first, motivation might carry us, but obstacles—whether external distractions or internal resistance—will inevitably arise. The key is to recognize that new behaviors take time before they solidify into habits. A routine doesn't become second nature overnight; it requires patience, persistence, and a willingness to push through discomfort. Just like building physical strength or mastering a skill, consistency is what ultimately transforms an intentional action into an effortless habit. There will be days when progress feels slow or when we falter, but the important thing is to return—again and again—to the practice. Over time, the struggle fades, and what once felt like effort becomes an integral, natural part of daily life.

EMPOWER YOUR PRACTICE:

The Habit Tracker!

This monthly tracker, found under "Accountability Tools,"
allows you to track up to 20 items daily. Get a visual
representation of specific habits you want to hold yourself
accountable for and monitor current habits.
Include your daily meditation on this list!

Chapter 4

Tools for Transformation

"If you want something you've never had, you must be willing to do something you've never done."

— Unknown

Transformation doesn't happen all at once. It's built through small choices—ones we make every day, especially when things feel messy or uncertain. This chapter offers tools outside of meditation to help you shift your mindset with a variety of practices to inspire your process. Come back to them whenever you need.

Use the Law of Attraction to Set the Narrative

Decide ahead of time that meditation is something you genuinely look forward to. This simple shift builds powerful momentum. One way to support your practice is by using the Law of Attraction, a teaching popularized by Abraham-Hicks, which says that what you consistently focus on—especially with strong emotion—shapes what you attract into your life. So, rather than approaching meditation as something you *have* to do, focus on how you *want* to feel. Visualize yourself as someone who meditates daily, and strengthen that identity with affirmations like, "I look forward to my meditation practice." When your mindset and emotions align with what you want, the practice begins to feel more natural, joyful, and even magnetic.

Meet Resistance

Do you feel a twinge of resistance when you think about meditating? This reaction could be shaped by past experiences, rigid expectations, or assumptions about what your practice *should* look like. Feelings of resistance tend to arise when something is out of alignment. Sometimes, resistance is emotional—rooted in self-doubt, guilt, or discouragement. Other times, it's more practical—the time no longer aligns, the lighting in the room is off, or sitting is uncomfortable.

Resistance isn't a roadblock; rather, it is a fork in the road offering a choice for a smoother path forward. When we pause and explore what's behind the discomfort, we gain the insight we need to move forward with more ease and clarity.

Find the Source

Take a moment to sit with any resistance you may have around meditation. Close your eyes and find the source of this feeling. Ask yourself each question, feel into the center of the discomfort, and see what arises. Whatever comes up, meet it with curiosity rather than criticism.

Ask yourself:

- Do I hold beliefs about meditation that don't feel good?
- What is discouraging me from practicing daily?
- Do I feel guilty for not starting—or for not sticking with it?

What came up?

_____

_____

As resistance arises in your practice, feel free to come back and use the following questions to check in. As above, ask yourself each question, feel into the center of the discomfort, and see what arises. Whatever comes up, meet it with curiosity rather than criticism.

What feels off?

_____

_____

What isn't supportive anymore?

_____

_____

Is there a small change I can make—a new perspective, a new habit, a new approach?

_____

_____

EMPOWER YOUR PRACTICE:

The War of Art

When I feel unmotivated or disconnected from my practice or writing, I pick up the book *The War of Art: Break Through the Blocks and Win Your Inner Creative Battles*. In this short and easy-to-read book, Steven Pressfield uncovers and dissects the nature of resistance and our relationship to it. His powerful perspectives, storytelling, and insights reach that place that feels untouchable. It often shakes me out of stagnation and remind me that moving forward is not just possible, but inevitable. If you need a soul-level pep talk, I highly recommend getting a copy!

Permission Slip

This is your permission slip to give yourself GRACE. You are on your journey, moving in *your* timing. Honor where you have been and know that in each moment, you can change the narrative.

PERMISSION SLIP

FOR: _____

You have full permission to release any guilt, shame, or regret tied to past decisions and behaviors. You were doing the best you could with the knowledge and awareness you had at the time. You deserve grace, compassion, and understanding. Every experience — good or bad — has been part of your growth, shaping you into the person you are today. You are not defined by your past but by how you choose to move forward.

You are worthy. You are allowed to evolve. Carry the lessons, release the weight of self judgment. Step into the present moment with kindness and self acceptance.

With love and understanding,

— *Your Higher Self*

Shift Your Thoughts

Thoughts are running through us constantly, most of them by default. When we become aware of a thought we do not want to have, an opportunity to make a change arises. All we have control over in each moment is our thoughts and our responses to our environment. Dr. Joe Dispenza, a self-help author and speaker who blends neuroscience and quantum physics to show how meditation can help us shift our energy, says, "If we want to change some aspect of our reality, we have to think, feel, and act in new ways; we have to 'be' different in terms of our responses to experiences." For example, we can't change the fact that we have to go to work each day, but we can change the way we approach it. Each moment invites us to choose a new way of thinking and being.

To truly embody a new thought, it helps to first identify why an undesirable or "bad" thought is present and then release our attachment to it. By recognizing we no longer want to think or respond a certain way, we invite an alternative thought to come in.

Take going to work for example: If you wake up with a feeling of dread each morning, see what it feels like to replace that with gratitude. Bring to the surface all of the reasons why you are grateful for your job. Maybe you like your co-workers, you believe in the work you do, or you like the color of the paint on the wall. Maybe you are grateful for the resources to enjoy yourself outside of work, to have food to eat, and to meet your basic needs. When an undesired thought slips in, catch it. Then, immediately shift to one of gratitude.

It may feel forced at first, but eventually your thoughts will naturally flow in the direction of your guidance. Know that the

truth lies in your desire to shift, and your belief that it is possible seals the deal.

Segment Intending

Abraham Hicks, a name associated with teachings on the Law of Attraction and the influence of mindset, has a powerful practice called Segment Intending used to deliberately choose your focus and desired outcome. Essentially, in each moment, you choose how the next one will unfold and how you will feel about it.

For example:

- When my co-worker walks into my office, I am not going to be annoyed.
- When I give my speech, I will be confident and convincing.
- When I talk to a friend about a boundary they crossed, I will be kind and compassionate, and they will be receptive.

- When I go to the store, I will have a pleasant experience and find everything I need.
- When I sit down for my meditation practice, I will feel relaxed and be present.

The idea is that by setting your intention, you align your energy, stay present, and create more positive experiences. The trick is *knowing* that this will be your reality before it happens. Tune into the feeling you want to have, and the Law of Attraction takes care of the rest.

Why Practice?

The reasons that drew you to meditation are the same ones that will reinforce your commitment to show up each day. They may fall into these categories:

1. Physical benefits
2. Mental benefits
3. Spiritual advancement
4. Positive qualities you want to attain
5. Behaviors you want to establish
6. Patterns you want to shift

Take a few moments to think about these and list them out.

I want to meditate daily to...

1 _____

2 _____

3 _____

4 _____

5 _____

6 _____

7 _____

8 _____

9 _____

10 _____

Examples:

I want to meditate daily to...

1. Release tension in my body (*physical benefit*)
2. Sleep more soundly (*physical benefit*)
3. Have a clearer mind throughout the day (*mental benefit*)
4. Improve my memory (*mental benefit*)
5. Receive guidance from intuition or spirit (*spiritual benefit*)
6. Connect with my true nature (*spiritual benefit*)
7. Be more patient (*positive quality I want to attain*)

8. Be more disciplined in achieving my goals (*pattern I want to shift*)

9. Live more intentionally (*behavior I want to establish*)

10. Spend less time on social media and streaming (*pattern I want to shift*)

Chapter 5

Accountability Support Systems

"All progress takes place outside the comfort zone."

— Michael John Bobak

Outside accountability provides valuable support in maintaining a daily practice. Meditation, like any habit, is easier to sustain when there's a sense of shared commitment. A meditation partner offers mutual encouragement, while an accountability partner helps reinforce consistency by checking in regularly. A book club or online community opens a deeper opportunity for learning, discussion, and motivation, making the practice feel more connected and less isolating. Knowing that others are on the same journey inspires dedication, provides new insights, and makes the process more engaging and fulfilling.

A Meditation Partner

Start the 42-day meditation commitment with a friend, a partner, or a roommate. Having someone to hold you accountable, or better yet, do it with you, goes a long way in staying motivated and on track. A meditation partner serves as an accountability companion by offering support, encouragement, and shared commitment to practicing daily.

Here are some ideas of what that looks like:

- Read your commitment letters to each other
- Send a quick "done" message after each session
- Set up daily or weekly check-ins to share challenges, reflections, or insights
- Celebrate small wins with a special dinner or treat after each 7-day streak
- Plan a celebratory dinner or activity to mark the completion of all 42 days

An Accountability Partner

An accountability partner helps keep your meditation practice on track by providing encouragement, check-ins, and a sense of shared commitment. By regularly touching base—whether through messages, calls, or in-person meetings—you create a structure that reinforces consistency. They remind you of your intentions, celebrate your progress, and offer support when you need it. Knowing that someone is invested in your practice adds a layer of responsibility, making it easier to stay committed. Choose a friend to share your commitment with and ask them to be your accountability partner. Here are some ideas of what that looks like:

- Read your commitment letter to each other
- Send a quick "done" message after each session
- Set up daily or weekly check-ins to share challenges, reflections, or insights from your practice
- Celebrate small wins with a special dinner or treat after each 7-day streak
- Plan a celebratory dinner or activity to mark the completion of all 42 days

M4T Journal Book Club

Get a few friends and commit together! Meet once every week or two to reflect on your progress and offer one another support and encouragement. Meet either in person, on the phone, or over a video call.

What Does an M4T Book Club Look Like?

- Share reflections on the week's practice
- Explore a theme or offer discussion topics
- Set personal goals
- Practice as a group

Ideas for Discussion Topics

- How conscious breathing affects the mind and body
- Developing awareness of thoughts without attachment
- Using meditation to process emotions
- Bringing mindfulness into daily routines
- How meditation helps with emotional regulation
- Speaking and listening with awareness
- What does it truly mean to be here now?

- Understanding impermanence in meditation
- Who are we beyond thoughts and identity?
- What blocks us, and how to move through it

M4T Online Community

The Meditation for Transformation Community serves as a powerful source of accountability, inspiration, and support for maintaining a consistent practice. Seeing others' dedication often reinforces our commitment, and encouraging others can help keep us motivated.

Connect and Get Inspired By

- Knowing others are practicing alongside you
- Publicly sharing progress (or struggles)
- Success stories and shared experiences
- Techniques, books, and tool recommendations
- Asking questions and receiving support

Join the private group today and start connecting with like-minded individuals who want to see you succeed!

Scan the Code or Follow the Link to Join the M4T Community.

https://www.facebook.com/groups/m4tcommunity

Chapter 6

Accountability Tools

"At any moment, you have a choice that either leads you closer to your spirit or further away from it."

— Thich Nhat Hanh

Accountability tools support your meditation practice by helping you stay consistent, track progress, and reflect on your journey. Documenting thoughts, feelings, and daily experiences in the journal pages enables deeper insights into your practice while reinforcing your commitment. The habit tracker offers a visual reminder to stay on course, helping build momentum and accountability. Together, these tools empower you to cultivate a sustainable and engaging practice.

Journal Pages Explained

These pages are your support system and accountability partner. Use them to track what is working well and explore what could be better in each practice. Daily entries include tools to track logistics, such as what practice you are doing and when, as well as lines to reflect on your personal experience and progress.

In the first week or two, it may be challenging to sit for 15 minutes and also take time for reflection. Note these in your entries. By the end of two weeks, you'll have 14 pages of reflections—a tangible reminder of your commitment to the practice and proof that you are showing up and following through. Celebrate this progress—it's a powerful step on your journey!

Over time, you begin to notice shifts within yourself and in your practice. Use these journal pages to capture both moments of frustration and success. Remember, the challenges you face now eventually make way for breakthroughs, and your reflections can help you see how far you've come. You've got this—each step, no matter how small, is a step forward.

Individual Log Items

- **Beginning of Practice Check-in:** Note how you feel by circling a number from 1 to 10.
- **Date**: Write down the day's date. If you skip a day, skip a page.
- **Time**: Record the time you start practicing.
- **Duration**: Record how long you practiced for. Include any time spent on your mat stretching, doing breath exercises, or preparing additional guided meditations. If you give up halfway through, be

honest - we have all done it. If you sit for an additional
10 minutes, great! Write this down, too.

- **Meditation Practice**: Write the technique or guided meditation used.
- **Posture**: How did you sit? Did you use any props? Were you comfortable?
- **Reflection**: Use the "Journal Entry" lines to write down your experience.
- What was your mind doing?
- Could you relax and get comfortable?
- Did you experience any physical sensations in your body?
- Did you think of anyone, or did you have an unexpected idea?
- Did you feel or experience anything else?
- **End of Practice Check-in:** Note how you feel by circling a number from 1 to 10.

Scan the Code or Follow the Link to Access
Additional Journal Pages

Sample Page

Daily Meditation Log   *- Day 1 -*

Start of the session (Circle one)

1   2   3   4   5   6   7   8   9   10

Distracted / Unable to drop in   Calm and Relaxed   Connection to Oneness/ Bliss

Date _____

Time: _____

Duration: _____

"The only person you should try to be better than is the person you were yesterday."
— Unknown

Meditation Practice: _____

Posture: _____

Journal Entry

_____

_____

_____

_____

_____

_____

_____

_____

_____

_____

_____

_____

_____

_____

_____

End of the session (Circle one):

1   2   3   4   5   6   7   8   9   10

Distracted / Unable to drop in   Calm and Relaxed   Connection to Oneness/ Bliss

Habit Tracker

Are you a list maker who gets a euphoric sensation checking off items on a to-do list? If so, this monthly Habit Tracker is your new guilt-free pleasure. As someone who feels a deep sense of accomplishment seeing a visual account of my achievements, this tool was key in establishing my daily practice.

Personalize the chart by choosing up to 20 items to track daily. Track anything from taking supplements and drinking water, to working out and limiting screen time. Get as creative as you want! Color the boxes in with different colored markers, or even use stickers to tick your boxes. Obviously, don't forget to include "15-minute meditation" on that list!

How to Use the Habit Tracker

Primary Goals: Start by committing to one or two new habits. List these at the top of your tracker. Aim to check them off daily.

Secondary Goals: These are additional activities you want to be aware of. Some days you may get all of them, and others only 30% of them.

Commonly Tracked Items

Wellness Habits

- Fitness activity
- Diet choices
- Floss teeth
- Drink 64 oz of water
- Take supplements

Limit Screen Time

- Reduce video game use
- Watch only __ minutes of streaming
- Limit social media to __ minutes

Alcohol / Caffeine

- Avoid alcohol on weekdays
- No coffee after noon

Information Consumption

- Limit exposure to news
- Listen to a podcast

Skill Development

- Practice an instrument
- Learn a second language

Other Ideas to Consider

Include low-hanging fruit

It feels good to have easy, quick tasks to complete each day and build momentum. I always include "take supplements in a.m." and "take supplements in p.m."

Try Habit Stacking

In Atomic Habits, James Clear introduces "habit stacking"—a method of building new habits by linking them to existing ones. By anchoring a desired behavior to something you already do, like meditating right after making coffee, the new habit becomes easier to remember and repeat.

Be realistic with your goals

Start small with new habits. Try "no sugar" and/or "no alcohol" instead of "new diet." Instead of "go to the gym," try "20 squats" or "a 20-minute walk." Small steps lead to lasting change.

Don't Expect 100% Every Day

You won't be at 100% every day, and that's okay. Honor your energy's ebb and flow, celebrate your progress, and be gentle with yourself—even when it looks different than expected.

Most importantly, don't take it too seriously!

Your tracker is a tool, not a contract. Use it to celebrate wins and spot areas for growth. If you miss things, it's part of life—focus on progress and adjust as needed.

Starting a New Month

Keep the following in mind as you reorganize and adjust your tracking sheet each month.

- As your primary focus items become second nature, start to transition secondary items into primary ones.
- Make changes that feel supportive. If it feels too overwhelming, you may risk abandoning the exercise altogether.
- As you find success, add other goals.
- Don't burn yourself out by taking on more than you can handle!

Habit Tracker Pages

Two blank trackers are included on the following pages.

Scan the code to download printable copies.

M4T Habit Tracker

Month _____

Habit	1	2	3	4	5	6	7	8	9	10	11	12	13	14	15	16	17	18	19	20	21	22	23	24	25	26	27	28	29	30	31
1																															
2																															
3																															
4																															
5																															
6																															
7																															
8																															
9																															
10																															
11																															
12																															
13																															
14																															
15																															

Notes: _____

_____

_____

*Use the QR code to track up to 20 habits

M4T Habit Tracker

Month _____

Habit	1	2	3	4	5	6	7	8	9	10	11	12	13	14	15	16	17	18	19	20	21	22	23	24	25	26	27	28	29	30	31
1																															
2																															
3																															
4																															
5																															
6																															
7																															
8																															
9																															
10																															
11																															
12																															
13																															
14																															
15																															

Notes: _____

*Use the QR code to track up to 20 habits

SHARE YOUR VOICE!

Light the Path for Someone Else

If this book has supported you in your meditation practice, even in small, quiet ways, **your story matters.**

There are so many people out there eager to begin their own journey to daily practice, but they don't know where to start. When you leave a review, you're not just sharing your opinion — you're lighting the way for someone else. You're saying, "This has helped me. It can help you too."

Your review doesn't have to be perfect or polished. Just a few honest words about how *Meditation for Transformation Journal* has supported you.

If you feel moved, you can leave a review on Amazon, Goodreads, or wherever you found the book. Thank you for being part of this journey.

Make a difference!
Scan the QR code and leave a review:

With deepest gratitude,
Rebekah Joy

Chapter 7

Getting Started

"Go inside and listen to your body, because your body will never lie to you. Your mind will play tricks, but the way you feel in your heart, in your guts, is the truth."

— Don Miguel Ruiz

These three paths provide support no matter where you are on your meditation journey—whether it's your first time meditating or you've been practicing for decades. Choose the one that best suits you.

Choose Your Path

- **Path One:** Fully Guided (Simplified)
- **Path Two:** Self-Guided (Modified)
- **Path Three:** Fully Modified

Path One: Fully Guided (Simplified)

Path One is for those seeking full structure and support. Days one through five follow the foundational meditations offered in Chapter 9 with access to pre-recorded guided meditations. Days six and seven offer options. On these days, you can either (1) re-listen to one of the guided meditations from days one through five, (2) guide yourself through a meditation from days one through five, or (3) explore a meditation from Chapter 10.

A self-guided meditation is where you lead yourself by memory through a meditation you've previously practiced without using an external voice or recording. If you can, read through the **Focus**, **How**, and **Practice Tips** and make the practice your own. Ignore the script completely and trust what arises. This practice helps cultivate your internal process.

Weekly Schedule:

- **Day 1:** Mindfulness Meditation: Passing Clouds
- **Day 2:** Grounding Meditation: Rooting to the Earth
- **Day 3:** Body Scan Meditation: Releasing Tension
- **Day 4:** Cultivating Gratitude Meditation (guided)
- **Day 5:** Visualization Meditation: Abundance
- **Days 6 & 7:** Re-listen to a guided meditation from days 1-5, self-guide a meditation from days 1-5, or explore a meditation from Chapter 10 (guided or self-guided)

Guidelines for Practice and Reflection:

- Before you begin each day, turn to the corresponding journal page and fill out the date and time, noting your overall well-being by circling a number between 1 and 10.
- Access guided meditation recordings via the QR code in Chapters 9 and 10.
- If using the recordings, no timer is necessary as they include an opening, guided practice, silent practice, and closing—all within 15 minutes.
- For self-guided meditations, set a timer for 15 minutes.
- After you finish each session, use that day's journal page to write out any reflections and circle a number between 1 and 10.

Path Two: Self-Guided (Modified)

Path Two is for those who prefer structure but want to self-guide their meditations using their own style. Following the same schedule as Path One, self-guide using your own techniques and meditations. You are also welcome to use any of the meditations offered in Chapters 9 and 10 or incorporate other meditation techniques you are comfortable with.

Weekly Schedule:

- **Day 1:** Mindfulness Meditation: Passing Clouds
- **Day 2:** Grounding Meditation: Rooting to the Earth
- **Day 3:** Body Scan Meditation: Releasing Tension
- **Day 4:** Cultivating Gratitude Meditation

- **Day 5:** Visualization Meditation: Abundance
- **Days 6 & 7**: Meditation of Your Choice

Guidelines for Practice and Reflection:

- Before you begin each day, turn to the corresponding journal page and fill out the date and time, noting your overall well-being by circling a number between 1 and 10.
- Guide yourself through your daily meditations, following the theme and techniques offered (or not).
- Explore the guided meditations, if you choose, using the QR codes in Chapters 9 and 10.
- For self-guided meditations, set a timer for 15 minutes.
- If using the recordings, no timer is necessary, as they include an opening, guided practice, silent practice, and closing—all within 15 minutes.
- After you finish each session, use that day's journal page to write out any reflections and circle a number between 1 and 10.

Path Three: Fully Modified

Path Three is for those who want the structure of the journal pages while using their own practices and techniques. If you already have a rich relationship with meditation, this path provides accountability tools to support a consistent daily practice while offering the freedom to lean into your experience.

Weekly Schedule:

Days 1-7: Meditation of Your Choice (self-guided)

Guidelines for Practice and Reflection:

- Before you begin each day, turn to the corresponding journal page and fill out the date and time, noting your overall well-being by circling a number between 1 and 10.
- Guide yourself through each meditation.
- Use a guided meditation (ideally 15 minutes or longer) that you are familiar with.
- Explore the meditations offered in this journal or choose your own.
- For self-guided meditations, set a timer for 15 or more minutes.
- If you're more experienced, consider committing to 20 or 30 minutes daily.

After you finish each session, use that day's journal page to write out any reflections and circle a number between 1 and 10.

Align and Prepare

Guided versus Self-Guided Meditations

To support the process of developing a personal practice, there is an option to self-guide a meditation of your choice or to repeat a prior meditation on days six and seven. In self-guided meditations, choose a guided meditation you have already done, and guide yourself through the process without using an external voice or recording. For support, read through the

Focus, **How**, and **Practice Tips** in Chapter 10. Don't get caught up in trying to recreate the script from memory. Rather, make the practice your own and trust the process.

Use of Music

While music is meditative, this daily practice is an invitation to be fully present with yourself. By focusing on silence, you gently observe whatever arises without external influences.

Explore Posture

Your comfort is essential. It might be the most important element of your practice. If sitting cross-legged in the middle of a room feels uncomfortable, you're less likely to show up for your sessions. Use this section to find a comfortable seat with whatever means necessary. That said, avoid lying down, as your body's natural tendency in that position is to doze off.

Find Your Seat

On the Floor:

- Sit on a cushion, blanket, yoga mat, or bolster
- Cross your legs in a way that feels natural
- Allow your feet and legs to rest on the floor
- Use a meditation bench if preferred
- Lean your back against the wall or use a floor chair (e.g., Back Jack, Nada Chair)

On a chair:

- Keep your feet flat on the ground, hip-width apart
- Position your knees at a 90-degree angle
- If the chair is too high, use a box or other support under your feet to maintain the 90-degree angle

- Sit upright without leaning against the chair's back
- If back support is needed, place a cushion or yoga block between your lower back and the chair

Seated Postures

  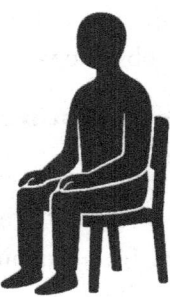

On the Floor
(Or on Cushion)   On a Meditation Stool   On a Chair

Sit with a Long Spine

- Allow your spine to be naturally straight without being rigid
- Imagine a string gently pulling the crown of your head upward

Relax Your Shoulders

- Drop your shoulders away from your ears
- Slightly lift your chest

Position Your Hands

- Rest your hands on your knees or lap, palms facing up or down
- Incorporate a mudra (hand gesture) if it is in your practice

Focus Your Head and Gaze

- Slightly tuck your chin or keep it parallel to the floor to maintain a neutral spine
- Meditate with your eyes open or closed: Closed eyes help you turn inward and block distractions, while a soft, unfocused gaze supports wakefulness and grounded awareness.
- If open, direct your gaze downward or between your eyebrows.
- If closed, relax your eyes or focus on the point between your eyebrows.

EMPOWER YOUR PRACTICE:

Props!

Do you need extra support to sit comfortably? Take a moment to look around your home for the perfect pillow, blanket, or yoga block. If those don't work, search online for other options. If something like a Back Jack catches your eye, consider purchasing it. Or, see if you can borrow one from a friend to test it out before purchasing.

Create a Meditation Space

Enhance your experience by creating a dedicated area to practice. The place where you meditate is your sanctuary. As you associate this area with mindfulness and ease, it encourages your body and mind to drop into a meditative state more naturally.

When choosing a place to meditate, consider:

- **Level of privacy**: A room or a corner where you can sit undisturbed
- **Comfort**: A place that feels good to be in
- **Distractions**: Somewhere with minimal distractions
- **Ambiance**: Light a candle, hang affirmations, or make a personal altar

When to Start

There is no pressure to start when you first get this journal. Before you officially begin, consider reading the first few chapters. These outline how to prepare and will set you up for success. When you are ready, choose the official start date. Starting on a Monday may be convenient calendar-wise. Or, starting on the first day of the New Year or a birthday may hold more personal significance. Whenever it is, the choice is up to you!

Chapter 8

Making the Commitment

"Are you paralyzed with fear? That's a good sign. Fear is good. Like self-doubt, fear is an indicator. Fear tells us what we have to do. Remember one rule of thumb: the more scared we are of a work or calling, the more sure we can be that we have to do it."

— Steven Pressfield, The War of Art

The most powerful choice you can make is to commit to yourself, your family, your community, and a higher power to start a daily practice. By embarking on this journey, you choose to step into the best version of yourself, not just to improve the quality of your own life but also to improve how you show up for others and the world around you.

Reflect on Your Intentions

Refer to the "Tools for Transformation" chapter, section "Look Forward to Your Practice" to revisit why a daily practice is important for you. If you have not filled this out yet, do so now to bring focus to writing and signing the letter.

Write Your Commitment Letter

You can keep this as simple as signing the commitment letter below or make it as personal and intentional as you'd like. This section includes several letter options along with meaningful practices for writing and signing your commitment.

Choose your letter format:

1. **General Commitment Letter:** If this letter feels complete, fill in the missing pieces and adopt it as your own.
2. **Personalized Commitment Letter**: Use this letter to fill in specific commitments to self, community, etc.
3. **Personal Commitment Letter:** Use this letter format if you prefer to create a letter entirely with your own words. Either use the lined page provided or a separate sheet.

Sign Your Letter:

Once complete, sign your letter. What you choose to do with it next is entirely up to you. Here are some suggestions:

1. **Revisit the letter.** When you need encouragement, open your journal and re-read it as a reminder of why your practice is important to you.
2. **Read the letter to your accountability partner.** If you choose to have an accountability partner, read them your letter. Being witnessed in this way invites a deeper sense of responsibility in keeping your commitment.
3. **Meditate with it.** Before each session, read your letter as an affirmation of your practice. If it is supportive, tear it out and place it in front of you each time.
4. **Release your commitment to the Universe.** Once your letter is signed, release it into the cosmos in a fire ceremony. Do this exercise outside where the smoke can carry your intentions to the cosmos, and the ashes are absorbed into the earth. Make the ceremony as elaborate or simple as you like: Burn it in a bonfire or fire pit at home, or use a candle or a lighter. The most important elements are your presence and intention.

A few tips for burning:

- Be sure to burn the letter in its entirety.
- Make sure the fire is contained.
- Stay with the fire until it goes out completely.
- Scatter the ashes in the wind, or cover them with dirt.

GENERAL COMMITMENT LETTER

To: My Higher Self, Community, Loved Ones, and Higher Power:

I _____ am writing this letter to commit to a daily meditation practice starting _____ .

This practice is important to me because:

_____

_____

My **Commitment to My Higher Self:** I dedicate time each day to meditate for___minutes to connect deeper with my inner wisdom and intuition, leading to self-discovery and personal growth.

My **Commitment to My Loved Ones:** I commit to a daily meditation practice so that I can be the best version of myself for my friends and family. I commit to showing up each day, and being present with what arises. The more self-love I cultivate, the more patient, understanding, and loving I am towards others.

My **Commitment to My Community:** I commit to meditating daily so I can be more of a support for my community. I recognize that when I prioritize my well-being, it directly impacts those around me, and I can be more present for those around me.

My **Commitment to a Higher Power:** I commit to practicing daily to connect with _____ [your higher power], seeking guidance and alignment with a higher, all-loving consciousness.

I remember this, and I remake this commitment each day. I am dedicated to integrating my daily meditation practice into my life. I know it will allow me to connect with my true nature, enrich my life, support my relationships, and connect with the world around me.

Sincerely,

_____   _____
[Sign Your Name]   Date

PERSONALIZED COMMITMENT LETTER

Date: _____

To: _____ ,

I am writing this letter to commit to starting and maintaining a daily meditation practice. This practice is important to me because:

_____

_____

Commitment to My Higher Self:

_____

_____

Commitment to My Community:

_____

_____

Commitment to My Family:

_____

_____

Commitment to a Higher Power:

I am dedicated to integrating this daily meditation practice into my life. I know it will allow me to connect with my true nature, enriching my life, my relationships, the world around me and

_____

_____

_____

_____

Sincerely,

_____

[Sign Your Name]

PERSONAL COMMITMENT LETTER

Date: _____

To: _____ ,

_____
_____
_____
_____
_____
_____
_____
_____
_____
_____
_____
_____
_____
_____
_____
_____
_____
_____
_____
_____
_____

Sincerely,

_____

[Sign Your Name]

Chapter 9

Meditation Practices

"Until you make the unconscious conscious, it will direct your life and you will call it fate."

— Carl Jung

The following practices are the foundation for the six-week program. Set your timer for 15 minutes to self-guide, or use the provided audio recordings.

Access to Audio Recordings

You can access a folder with all the meditations from this journal by scanning the QR code or visiting the link in the "Supporting Resources" section. If you find the audible breaths distracting, alternate audio versions without them are also available in the same folder.

Scan for Audio Files:

Scan for YouTube Videos:

1. Mindfulness Meditation: Passing Clouds

- **Focus:** Present-moment awareness
- **How:** In a comfortable seated posture, focus on your breath. Observe thoughts, sensations, and emotions without judgment as they arise.
- **Practice Tip:** If your mind wanders, observe it happening as if you are an outsider looking in. Without attaching "good" or "bad" to the thought, simply bring your awareness back to your breath.

Script:

"Close your eyes. Allow your hands to rest face down on your legs.

As you inhale, feel your spine lengthen. On the exhale, soften your shoulders.

Become aware of your breath. Notice its natural rhythm flowing in and out of your body. **[Two full breaths]**

Feel the sensation of air entering your nostrils, filling your lungs, and then gently leaving your body. **[Two full breaths]**

Without changing a thing, observe the length of the inhale and the length of the exhale. **[Two full breaths]**

Feel the breath anchoring you in this moment. **[Four full breaths]**

As you breathe, become aware of any thoughts that arise. As if from the outside looking in, just notice them without judgment or attachment. **[Three full breaths]**

Imagine each thought as a passing cloud, drifting by in a clear blue sky and then dissolving into the horizon. **[Three full breaths]**

If your mind wanders, gently guide your attention back to your breath and back to the clear blue sky. **[Three full breaths]**

As thoughts arise, allow them to drift by without judgment. **[Three full breaths]**

Watch as they float and then dissolve into the vastness of the sky. **[Six full breaths]**

As other thoughts arise, notice them without being attached to them. **[Three full breaths]**

Each time a thought takes you off course, return to the breath. **[Three full breaths]**

When all thoughts dissolve, lean into the clear expanse of the sky. **[Three full breaths]**

Continue like this: observing and dissolving thoughts. **[Thirty full breaths]**

As thoughts continue to dissolve, rest in the expanse before you. **[Forty full breaths]**

Deepening your inhale, bring your awareness back to your body.

On the exhale feel your connection to the surface below you.

[Two full breaths]

Without opening your eyes, become aware of the space around you. **[Two full breaths]**

Notice any sensations that arise in your body, then allow them to settle. **[Two full breaths]**

Take a moment to notice what positive qualities surfaced: stillness, compassion, spaciousness. Whatever comes up for you, invite these qualities to stay with you throughout the day.

When you're ready, allow the eyes to open. As light pours in, slowly look around you, noticing, as if for the first time."

2. Grounding Meditation: Rooting to the Earth

- **Focus:** Grounding, connection with the earth
- **How:** In a comfortable seat, imagine roots growing from the base of your spine or feet, reaching deep into the earth. Feel the stability and strength of the earth below you, drawing energy up through the roots into your body.
- **Practice Tip**: If you feel distracted, gently reconnect with the sensation of your roots.
  - Visualize them growing deeper, offering support and balance with each breath.
  - Explore the meditation in a standing posture, feet rooted to the earth.
  - For tips on recording the script in your own voice refer back to Chapter 2 under "Support Materials."

Script:

"Close your eyes. Take a deep breath in. Feel your spine lengthen as you inhale, lifting through the crown of your head. On the exhale, bring your awareness to the skin and bones holding you. Feel the weight of your body supported by the ground beneath you. **[Two full breaths]**

Inhale deeply through the nose, and feel the chest expand and open. As you exhale, release any tension and settle more deeply.

[Two full breaths]

Feel the foundation of your legs and feet. Notice a softness as

they touch the floor. Relax more with each breath. **[Two full breaths]**

Feel where your body connects to the earth below. Notice a small taproot growing from you and going into the earth. As it grows downward, watch as smaller roots grow and fan out like a web below. **[Four full breaths]**

Allow your roots to go deeper and deeper into the rich soil. **[Two full breaths]**

Feel how the earth rises to meet you; notice how she cradles each tentacle in her cool touch. **[Two full breaths]**

As your roots continue to go down into the earth, feel yourself absorb the nutrients of the rich soil. **[Two full breaths]**

Continue to draw this energy in and up, and feel it spread through your legs, nourishing your entire body. **[Four full breaths]**

As it enters the base of your spine, feel stability, strength, and vitality flowing up from the earth. Feel these roots anchor you firmly to the ground. **[Four full breaths]**

As it flows to the navel, notice how safe and supported you are. **[Four full breaths]**

Feel the energy flood through the upper abdomen. Notice an inner strength radiating from within. **[Four full breaths]**

Take a few breaths, absorbing the flow of energy from the earth.

Continue to draw it in through your roots. Feel the earth amplify and support you. **[Sixteen full breaths]**

Bring your awareness to your sit bones or your feet, following the roots down through the ground. As you follow your roots, send gratitude back into the earth. **[Eight full breaths]**

Think of all of the ways she supports you. Continue to offer gratitude as these thoughts rise. **[Twelve full breaths]**

Take a deep breath in, and sweep your hands into the sky like the branches of a tree. From the tips of your branches, feel your connection to the earth down through your roots. Expand your branches into the sky just as your roots expand into the earth. **[Four full breaths]**

Bring your palms together and allow them to float down to your heart center. Gently press your hands together in gratitude as you lean into your connection with the earth. **[Two full breaths]**

Slowly open your eyes, taking a few moments to soak in your surroundings. Feel the connection at your feet.

Continue to visualize these roots growing into the ground, knowing that you are always supported and nurtured by the earth beneath you."

3. Body Scan Meditation: Releasing Tension

- **Focus:** Deep relaxation and body awareness
- **How:** In a comfortable seated posture, bring your awareness to each part of your body. Start at the head and slowly make your way down to the toes. Invite each body part to release tension. Notice any imbalances or emotions that arise.

- **Practice Tips:**
  - Practice lying down for full relaxation, but stay awake.
  - When you notice tension, breathe into that area before moving on.
  - For tips on recording the script in your own voice, refer back to Chapter 2 under "Support Materials."

Script:

"Settle into your body. Close your eyes and allow a sliver of light to come through, or close them completely. Bring your inner gaze to the space between your eyebrows. Notice how your inner awareness shifts. Gently lift the chest and relax the shoulders. Feel your spine supporting you. Soften any tension.

Breathe in through the nose. Feel the air fill your entire body, expanding to the edges of your skin. **[Three full breaths]**

Through the mouth, exhale and release any heaviness or tension. **[Three full breaths]**

Bring your attention to your entire head, jaw, cheekbones, ears, and nose. Notice any sensations present: lightness or heaviness, warmth or cold. Without labeling "good" or "bad," see what you feel. **[Two full breaths]**

On each exhale, find softness and ease. **[Two full breaths]**

Shift your awareness to your neck and shoulders. What sensations are present? Notice what you feel. **[Two full breaths]**

Use the breath to dissolve any tension. **[Two full breaths]**

Come to your center, and feel your chest and upper back. Become aware of any lightness or heaviness, expansion or contraction. **[Four full breaths]**

Glide your awareness down your arms to your palms and fingertips, noticing and then relaxing. **[Four full breaths]**

Feel your belly, lower back, and pelvis. As the breath fills, notice what is present. Let go of any constriction or holding. Invite a sensation of weightlessness. **[Four full breaths]**

Continue to the thighs and the knees, noticing and releasing. **[Four full breaths]**

Coming to the calves and the ankles: become aware of any sensations and then release them. **[Four full breaths]**

Moving to the feet and toes, notice what arises and then allow it to dissolve with the breath. **[Four full breaths]**

Now, become aware of your entire body. Notice any overall sensations. Release any residual tension that remains. **[Eight full breaths]**

Continue to invite the clearing quality of your breath to soften any imbalances. Watch the imbalances dissolve into the space beneath you. **[Sixteen full breaths]**

Bring your awareness back to your body. Notice the rise and fall of the belly, your connection to the floor, and the feeling of your clothes against your skin. **[Four full breaths]**

With the next breath, invite a gentle warmth to fill your entire being. Draw in warmth on the inhale, and expand into a state of ease on the exhale. **[Two full breaths]**

Focus the warmth on any places that feel out of balance. **[Four full breaths]**

Bring your awareness to your posture. Gently drop your chin to your chest and make slow circles with your neck. **[One full breath]** Switch directions. **[One full breath]**

Come to your center, and when you are ready, open your eyes.

With your eyes open, tune into your body. Notice the quality of ease, and invite it to be with you as you move through the day."

4. Cultivating Gratitude Meditation

- **Focus:** Cultivate a sense of gratitude.
- **How:** Inhale deeply, bringing your awareness to the present moment. As you exhale, silently acknowledge something in your life that you are grateful for. Continue to breathe slowly and deeply, expanding your sense of gratitude with each breath.
- **Practice Tips:**
  - As you inhale, visualize the gratitude filling you; as you exhale, send this gratitude outward.
  - If your mind drifts, gently return your focus to the breath or to the gratitude you're cultivating.

Script:

"Gently close your eyes, and allow your mind to settle into this moment. Take a few deep, grounding breaths. Tapping once

again into the roots that connect you to the earth. **[Two full breaths]**

Inhale through the nose. Feel the air fill your lungs. Exhale through your mouth, feeling a lightness overcome your body. **[Two full breaths]**

Visualize your body in its entirety. As if looking in from the outside, notice in awe how its daily functions support your well-being. **[Four full breaths]**

Think of the strength and stamina it offers in completing daily tasks. What specific examples come to mind? Offer your body gratitude for these. **[Four full breaths]**

Think of its ability to consume food, absorb nutrients, and fuel you. Offer your body gratitude for these. **[Four full breaths]**

Become aware of your body's resilience. Its ability to recover from injuries, challenges, and stress. Its ability to restore itself in sleep. Thank your body for its healing ability. **[Four full breaths]**

With a sense of awe, consider the wisdom of your body and its natural rhythms: its heartbeat, digestion, and breath. Unconscious functions that support your life even when you do not notice them: Bring your attention to them now. **[Two full breaths]**

Now, visualize your life as a whole. Reflect on the gift of your existence and your journey so far. Feel gratitude for being alive in this moment. **[Two full breaths]**

Think of the structures in place that support you—where you live and your mode of transportation. Offer gratitude for the shelter and mobility they allow. **[Two full breaths]**

Acknowledge the work you do, your creativity, and the skills that allow you to provide for yourself or others. Even if you seek a change, thank these opportunities for supporting you now. **[Four full breaths]**

Think of someone who supports you or inspires you. See them sitting in front of you, smiling. Offer your gratitude by sharing the ways they show up and are present for you. **[Four full breaths]**

Consider a challenge you faced in your life and the lessons you learned. **[Two full breaths]**

Think about how this has shaped who you are today. Thank the part of the experience that brought growth and a new perspective. **[Two full breaths]**

Feel your gratitude expand like a warm light wrapping itself around you. With each inhale, feel the light growing brighter and warmer. As you exhale, feel it expanding outwards, touching every corner of your being. Let this light of gratitude fill you, enveloping your body and mind. **[Eight full breaths]**

Now, visualize the future you desire- the one that lies ahead of you. **[Two full breaths]**

How does it feel? Take a few breaths to explore what it feels like to fully live this future. **[Four full breaths]**

In what ways is it currently unfolding in your life? **[Two full breaths]**

Offer gratitude for the unfolding of this future. Trust and know that you are worthy of it. **[Eight full breaths]**

Allow this gratitude, for yourself, for the people in your life, and for experiences to flow freely through you, expanding beyond the people you know. Imagine it encompassing all beings around the world, from your community to the entire planet. Send the light of this gratitude outward. Feel it link and connect with all life. **[Four full breaths]**

Now, bring your awareness back to the room; feel your gratitude radiating outward. **[Two full breaths]**

Feel content with what you have right now. **[Two full breaths]**

How will you continue to live in this gratitude? What small acts can you offer to yourself or others? **[Two full breaths]**

Think of one small thing you can do today and commit to it now. **[Two full breaths]**

As you come back, start to notice any sounds around you. When you're ready, gently open your eyes. Look around the room, shining the light of your gratitude on your surroundings."

5. Visualization Meditation: Abundance

- **Focus:** Use mental imagery to cultivate a sense of abundance and appreciation.
- **How:** Visualize yourself in a peaceful, expansive environment— perhaps a lush forest, open meadow, or sunset shoreline. Let the scene reflect the fullness of your life. Notice the colors, textures, and shapes that surround you. Imagine each element as a symbol of something abundant in your life.

- **Practice Tips:**
  - Engage all five senses: What do you see, hear, smell, feel, or even taste?
  - If your focus drifts or the image fades, gently guide yourself back by recreating the scene detail by detail.
  - Let your breath help anchor you in the visualization.

Script:

"Close your eyes, and tune in to your breath. Allow the chest to rise and fall in its natural rhythm. Follow the air as it enters through the nose and fills the belly. On the inhale, feel yourself become taller, chest opening. On the exhale, feel your body relax and become heavy. **[Two full breaths]**

Imagine that you are standing on the threshold of the most beautiful garden expanding as far as you can see: beds of vibrantly colored vegetables, orchards of fruit trees flow over hillsides, endless rows of corn trellised with beans and woven with squash, berry bushes and nut trees are so ripe that the fruit falls to the ground. **[Four full breaths]**

Take a moment to look around. What else is growing in this garden? **[Four full breaths]**

On the edges of the garden, a vibrant stream is fed by fresh mountain springs. Beyond this garden, a forest rises on mountainsides, trees reaching into the purest, clean air, touching the edges of the sky as it expands in soft pinks and blues above. **[Four full breaths]**

As you look closer, notice the garden being tended. Men and women, young children and elders, people of all colors and backgrounds, together bathing in abundance. Taking only what they need, and yet there is more than enough. Take a moment to look around. Who do you see tending the garden? What are they doing? **[Four full breaths]**

Now, take a bird's eye view. Feel yourself soaring above the garden and the ridges. As you rise higher and higher, notice that this is one of many gardens. Explore the earth's abundance, see it pouring out of every crevice of her body. **[Eight full breaths]**

On the next inhale, make your way back to the threshold of the garden. As you land on the ground, feel your feet softly touch the earth. Offer gratitude for the abundance the earth provides. **[Four full breaths]**

Bring your awareness to the abundance in the garden of *your* life. **[Four full breaths]**

What fruits do you water? What relationships do you tend to? **[Four full breaths]**

What areas of your life overflow with abundance? **[Four full breaths]**

Feel the abundance flow in and through you. **[Four full breaths]**

Take a deep breath in, bring your hands palm to palm at your heart-center, offering gratitude for the abundance in your life. **[Three full breaths]**

When you are ready, open your eyes. Take a moment to acknowledge and absorb the abundance that surrounds you. As you move through your day, bring your awareness to the abundance that flows in your life. Call it in, and continuously offer gratitude for the earth and all that is provided."

Chapter 10

Meditations for Transformation

"Awakening is not changing who you are, but discarding who you are not."

— Deepak Chopra

This section explores meditation practices that have deeply supported my journey. I share their origins and honor their background. These practices illuminate the transformational power of meditation by exploring deeper processes that lead to personal expansion and self-discovery.

Scan for Audio Files:

Scan for YouTube Videos:

Who Am I?

I unexpectedly experienced my first meditation practice while studying abroad in Seoul, South Korea. Drawn in by the exquisite blend of traditional and modern architecture, a friend and I wandered from the busy city street into a Buddhist temple named Beomnyeonsa. Browsing the English section of the temple's bookstore, we met Myo-Kyung Sunim, a resident Korean monk. His round, beaming smile illuminated the room as he approached me, a gray robe hanging on his frame like an oversized blanket. My friend, Ji Hyang, translated as he offered to take us on a tour of the temple, which we graciously accepted.

On Beomnyeonsa's third floor, we entered the main temple. Natural lighting awakened the technicolor murals that traversed the walls and then sprawled across the ceiling in intricate, hand-painted, linear designs. Five golden Buddhas, each about six feet high, sat on an elevated altar. With a life of their own, they shifted and smiled in the flickering candles at their feet. Sitting on meditation cushions front and center of the altar, Myo-Kyung asked if I knew how to meditate. When I said I did not, Ji Hyang translated as he led us through this practice together:

We sat comfortably on cushions, our legs crossed, eyes softly focused on a spot on the floor a few feet in front of us. Our gaze was slightly open to maintain a connection with the physical realm. The back of our hands rested on our knees, thumbs touching the tips of the middle finger. Myo-Kyung guided us in an internal exercise to calm the nervous system. We gently rolled the top of the tongue on the roof of the mouth in a wave motion. The soothing rhythm overtook me. I began to release the self-consciousness I felt about being the only non-Korean person in the temple and being front and center.

He guided us to focus on the question *"Who am I?"*

Ji Hyang said, "You have to genuinely ask the question with the desire to learn. You can't be afraid of the answer, no matter what it is." She said the components of the question change each time, and you learn something new. "By learning who we are, we learn who the Buddha was," Ji Hyang translated.

As I pondered this question, my body became weightless, and I watched my mind drift off with the incense. The three of us sat as if suspended in a lazy-eyed staring contest with the large gold Buddhas before us. Though nothing profound happened during that first meditation, I felt a peace and stillness growing inside of me.

In the months that followed, I visited the temple regularly and embraced the practice that Meo-Kyung Sunim shared. Sitting on the temple floor, I took in the breeze whirling in from the large open windows to dance with the smoke of the flickering candles. The silence felt alive, and the murals on the vaulted ceilings felt open to the sky. Sitting at the feet of the golden Buddhas, I continued to ask myself, "Who am I?"

As I asked this question, I watched parts of myself fall away. I learned that I was not my past. I was not my cynicism. I was not my guilt. I was not lonely. And when I asked myself again, "Who am I?" I remembered that I am the emptiness, and I am also joy. I am playfulness. I am gratitude, and I am divine love. When met with the desire to know, this simple technique taught me to meet myself where I was and that I could experience a peace that lay just beyond the busyness of my mind.

Who Am I Meditation

- **Focus:** Self-inquiry, dissolving the illusion of a separate self to reveal a deeper, formless awareness
- **How:** Find a quiet place without distractions to sit. Bring your attention inward. Silently or aloud, ask "Who am I?". Sit for a moment and observe what arises— thoughts, memories, identities. (e.g., "I am a teacher." "I am a friend"). Each time a thought or label appears, ask: "Who is aware of this?" Instead of seeking an intellectual answer, allow awareness itself to be your focus. As layers of identity fade, rest in the open space of pure awareness. Notice the presence that remains beyond roles and

thoughts—**this is your true self.** If your mind wanders, gently return to the question. After some time, let go of the question, and sit in silence and spaciousness.

- **Practice Tips:**
  - Don't chase answers—rest in the space between thoughts.
  - Focus on the feelings that arise.
  - Trust in the process, even if the prompts feel vague.

Script:

"Take a deep inhale. Exhale slowly. Feel the weight of your body resting on the floor. Allow your shoulders to relax and your jaw to soften. Feel your breath settle into a natural rhythm. **[Two full breaths]**

Shift your focus inward. Notice any sensations in your body. Follow the rise and fall of your breath. **[Two full breaths]**

Become aware of the thoughts passing through your mind. Observe what arises without judgment or attachment. **[Two full breaths]**

Now, bring your attention to your heart center. **[One full breath]**

To the core of who you are. **[One full breath]**

Connect to the source of your being. **[Two full breaths]**

Ask: "Who am I?" **[Two full breaths]**

Without searching for an answer, notice what arises. **[Four full breaths]**

Now ask: "What part of me is aware of this thought?" **[Two full breaths]**

Feel into the presence that is witnessing the thought. **[Four full breaths]**

Again, ask: "Who am I?" **[Two full breaths]**

Allow the answer to rise from the depths of your being. **[Two full breaths]**

Lean into the part of you that is aware of these thoughts as they arise. **[Two full breaths]**

Allow each answer to dissolve into the stillness. **[Two full breaths]**

When everything dissolves—what remains? **[Four full breaths]**

Continue to ask, "Who am I?" Notice what part of you responds,

and then allow the answer to dissolve. Rest in what remains. **[Twenty-four full breaths]**

What part of you is present, untouched, unchanging? Be with the stillness and silence.

There are no more questions, nothing to search for. Allow yourself to merge with the spaciousness and the presence within. **[Sixteen full breaths]**

Bring your awareness back to your body. Come back to your breath. Feel the softness of the ground beneath you. When you are ready, slowly open your eyes.

Gently look around, integrating back into the physical world.

With your eyes open, sense that part of you that is unchanging and always present."

Journal Prompts:

- What identities, ideas, or roles came up?
- Did they dissolve?
- How do I maintain a connection with the unchanging part of me?

Tending and Transforming Emotions

You know when you feel an emotion, and it takes over your entire day? Maybe a friend says something that hurts your feelings (pain), or you make a mistake at work (regret). There is a deadline that feels impossible to meet (fear) or pressure from a family member to do something (guilt). You attempt to move through the day as normal, but the feeling lingers like a raw wound, poking at you from the inside. Subconsciously you are consumed, stewing, and thinking in circles. As the tension builds throughout the day, or even over several weeks, you try to redirect your thoughts and even override them with better ones. But nothing works, and the feeling builds and builds. At the breaking point, you have no choice but to be with the feeling until it empties through tears, cries, rage, or shaking.

Despite the process outlined above, our emotions are working diligently to support us. They are our internal barometer and intuitive security system. We have no problem managing our emotional landscape when everything is going well, but most of us are never taught how to be with uncomfortable emotions. When we have the tools to work with them, these emotions are gateways to our expansion and growth, allowing us to tap into their wisdom before they take over.

In my 200-hour yoga teacher training at the Asheville Yoga Center, our lead instructor, Kimberley Puryear, shared a tool that was foundational in the development of this meditation. "When a difficult emotion surfaces," she said, "envision holding it like a baby in your arms. Allow yourself to be present with it; allow it to express itself fully. Respond with compassion and tenderness. Recognize that it is a part of you that wants to be seen."

The simple act of being with an emotion without judgment can create the shift needed for that emotion to dissolve. When we create space to sit with feelings like guilt or fear, we uncover deeper issues within us that need attention. For example, sometimes a hurtful comment from a roommate brings to light a belief we have about ourselves that is not true. Deep regret is an invitation to let go of the past, allowing us to be more aware in the future. We might find that feelings of guilt expose obligations we no longer want to be responsible for.

Whether an emotion has recently surfaced or has been lingering around for decades, meditation is a tool to facilitate a conversation. In the stillness and silence, we hold space for feelings to be fully expressed and witnessed. We invite their wisdom and aim to integrate any lessons learned.

Facing uncomfortable feelings takes courage. Darkness and the unknown are scary, but it's simply where we have yet to shine a light. In this meditation, we illuminate the parts of ourselves seeking to be revealed, discovering that the looming shadows are made by the smallest unknowns.

Holding Our Emotions Meditation

- **Focus**: Identify an emotion you want to transform, and sit with it fully.
- **How**: Invite the emotion to be present in your body. Allow yourself to experience the full range of feelings that arise. Visualize the emotion as a small child, and hold it in your arms. Allow it to yell, cry, and scream, to be a two-year-old and throw a tantrum. Permit it to fully express what it needs. Rock it in your arms like you would a baby, with the compassion and understanding of a mother. Allow the full spectrum of the emotion to move through you and be with it, however long it takes.
- **Practice Tips:**
  - Use this practice when an uncomfortable emotion arises.
  - Keep showing up. You may have to do this meditation many times before an emotion fully dissolves.
  - Once you feel a shift within, invite in a quality you want to replace that emotion with. If you release fear, maybe invite trust.

Script:

"Close your eyes. Take a deep breath in. Feel the belly and the chest rise. As you exhale, feel your body become heavy. **[Two full breaths]**

Become aware of your skin, your muscles, and your bones. Feel them supporting you.

Through the nose, breathe deeply. Exhale slowly and steadily. Release any tension. Allow the breath to be soft and natural. Feel the air flowing in and out. Feel your skin soften and your jaw relax.

Now bring your awareness to your center. Allow the emotion most alive in you to rise to the surface. **[Two full breaths]**

Invite the emotion to get stronger. Feel it build inside of you. **[Four full breaths]**

What is it like to feel it fully? **[Four full breath]**

What is the root of the emotion? **[Four full breath]**

Ask it. **[Four full breath]**

Is it fear or attachment? Anger or abandonment? Another emotion? **[Four full breath]**

Feel it in your body. Notice what sensations arise. What memories surface? **[Four full breath]**

Does it have a shape or form? A color or a vibration? **[Two full breaths]**

Why is it there? What does it want you to know? **[Four full breaths]**

Spend the next few breaths feeling into the emotion, and see what arises for you. **[Eight full breaths]**

Watch as the emotion becomes a small child. Scoop it up, and wrap it in your arms. Invite it to fully express itself. Let it cry, let it scream, let it yell, and release. **[Four full breaths]**

As it does, whisper gently, "It's okay. Let it out. I see you. You are okay. You are safe. I've got you." **[Four full breaths]**

Continue as long as needed, until the emotion releases and is fully expressed. **[Eight full breaths]**

When you feel the baby is calm in your arms, exhausted and complete, continue to rock and comfort it. Gently say, "Thank you for trying to protect me. Thank you for having my best interests in mind. I am listening. I trust you." Offer gratitude for any other insights or lessons that come through. **[Two full breaths]**

With compassion and tenderness, allow the baby - the emotion - to dissolve and be absorbed by the earth beneath you and the space around you.

When you feel complete, invite your breath to deepen. Bring your attention to where you sensed the emotion in your body. Tune into the spaciousness of your body. Invite a new quality to fill this space: love or compassion, trust or gratitude, or another emotion. **[One full breath]**

With each inhale, allow the new emotion to fill and expand within. Rest in the space of these new qualities. **[Eight full breaths]**

Notice the softness of your skin. Feel the strength of your body.

Invite movement into your fingers and toes. Rocking and stretching.

Bring your right hand to your heart and the left to your belly. Offer yourself gratitude. Acknowledge your ability to listen deeply and show up for yourself in this way.

When you are ready, allow your eyes to open very slowly.

Feel the spaciousness you created.

Feel yourself embody the new qualities you called in.

Make a conscious choice to carry them forward throughout your day."

Journal Prompts:

- What was the root of the emotion? Did this surprise me?
- Did the emotions take on a color or a shape?
- Did it reveal itself as a person I know or a part of myself?
- What are my biggest takeaways?
- How will I integrate what I've learned?

Chapter 11

Meditation Journal Pages

"Your work is to discover your work and then with all your heart to give yourself to it."

— Buddha

Daily Meditation Log

- *Day 1* -

Start of the session (Circle one)

1 2 3 4 5 6 7 8 9 10

Distracted / Unable to drop in   Calm and Relaxed   Connection to Oneness / Bliss

Date _____

Time: _____

Duration: _____

"The only person you should try to be better than is the person you were yesterday."
— Unknown

Meditation Practice: _____

Posture: _____

Journal Entry

_____

_____

_____

_____

_____

_____

_____

_____

_____

_____

_____

_____

_____

_____

_____

End of the session (Circle one):

1 2 3 4 5 6 7 8 9 10

Distracted / Unable to drop in   Calm and Relaxed   Connection to Oneness / Bliss

Daily Meditation Log

- Day 2 -

Start of the session (Circle one)

1　2　3　4　5　6　7　8　9　10

Distracted / Unable to drop in　　Calm and Relaxed　　Connection to Oneness / Bliss

Date _____

Time: _____

Duration: _____

Meditation Practice: _____

Posture: _____

"You have power over your mind not outside events. Realize this, and you will find strength."
— Marcus Aurelius

Journal Entry

_____

_____

_____

_____

_____

_____

_____

_____

_____

_____

_____

_____

_____

_____

_____

_____

_____

End of the session (Circle one):

1　2　3　4　5　6　7　8　9　10

Distracted / Unable to drop in　　Calm and Relaxed　　Connection to Oneness / Bliss

Daily Meditation Log

- Day 3 -

Start of the session (Circle one)

1 2 3 4 5 6 7 8 9 10

Distracted / Unable to drop in   Calm and Relaxed   Connection to Oneness / Bliss

Date _____

Time: _____

Duration: _____

Meditation Practice: _____

Posture: _____

"You will never be able to escape from your heart. So it is better to listen to what it has to say."
— Paulo Coelho

Journal Entry

_____

_____

_____

_____

_____

_____

_____

_____

_____

_____

_____

_____

_____

_____

_____

_____

_____

End of the session (Circle one):

1 2 3 4 5 6 7 8 9 10

Distracted / Unable to drop in   Calm and Relaxed   Connection to Oneness / Bliss

Daily Meditation Log

- Day 4 -

Start of the session (Circle one)

| 1 | 2 | 3 | 4 | 5 | 6 | 7 | 8 | 9 | 10 |

Distracted / Unable to drop in   Calm and Relaxed   Connection to Oneness / Bliss

Date: _____

Time: _____

Duration: _____

Meditation Practice: _____

Posture: _____

> "Living in the present moment
> creates the experience of eternity."
>
> — Deepak Chopra

Journal Entry

_____

_____

_____

_____

_____

_____

_____

_____

_____

_____

_____

_____

_____

_____

_____

_____

_____

End of the session (Circle one):

| 1 | 2 | 3 | 4 | 5 | 6 | 7 | 8 | 9 | 10 |

Distracted / Unable to drop in   Calm and Relaxed   Connection to Oneness / Bliss

Daily Meditation Log

Start of the session (Circle one)

🪷 🪷 🪷 🪷 🪷 🪷 🪷 🪷 🪷 🪷
1　2　3　4　5　6　7　8　9　10

Distracted / Unable to drop in　　Calm and Relaxed　　Connection to Oneness / Bliss

Date _____

Time: _____

Duration: _____

Meditation Practice: _____

Posture: _____

"All we have to decide is what to do
with the time that is given us."
— J.R.R. Tolkien,
The Fellowship of the Ring

Journal Entry

_____

_____

_____

_____

_____

_____

_____

_____

_____

_____

_____

_____

_____

_____

_____

End of the session (Circle one):

🪷 🪷 🪷 🪷 🪷 🪷 🪷 🪷 🪷 🪷
1　2　3　4　5　6　7　8　9　10

Distracted / Unable to drop in　　Calm and Relaxed　　Connection to Oneness / Bliss

Daily Meditation Log

- Day 6 -

Start of the session (Circle one)

🪷 🪷 🪷 🪷 🪷 🪷 🪷 🪷 🪷 🪷
1   2   3   4   5   6   7   8   9   10

Distracted / Unable to drop in   Calm and Relaxed   Connection to Oneness / Bliss

Date _____

Time: _____

Duration: _____

Meditation Practice: _____

Posture: _____

"What we are today comes from our thoughts of yesterday, and our present thoughts build our life of tomorrow: Our life is the creation of our mind." — Buddha

Journal Entry

_____

_____

_____

_____

_____

_____

_____

_____

_____

_____

_____

_____

_____

_____

_____

_____

End of the session (Circle one):

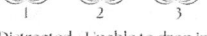

1   2   3   4   5   6   7   8   9   10

Distracted / Unable to drop in   Calm and Relaxed   Connection to Oneness / Bliss

Daily Meditation Log

- Day 1 -

Start of the session (Circle one)

1 2 3 4 5 6 7 8 9 10

Distracted / Unable to drop in   Calm and Relaxed   Connection to Oneness / Bliss

Date _____

Time: _____

Duration: _____

Meditation Practice: _____

Posture: _____

"The wound is the place where
the Light enters you."
— Rumi

Journal Entry

_____

_____

_____

_____

_____

_____

_____

_____

_____

_____

_____

_____

_____

_____

_____

_____

_____

End of the session (Circle one):

1 2 3 4 5 6 7 8 9 10

Distracted / Unable to drop in   Calm and Relaxed   Connection to Oneness / Bliss

Daily Meditation Log

- Day 1 -

Start of the session (Circle one)

🪷 🪷 🪷 🪷 🪷 🪷 🪷 🪷 🪷 🪷
1   2   3   4   5   6   7   8   9   10

Distracted / Unable to drop in   Calm and Relaxed   Connection to Oneness / Bliss

Date _____

Time: _____

Duration: _____

Meditation Practice: _____

Posture: _____

"Whatever happens around you, don't take it personally... Nothing other people do is because of you. It is because of themselves."
— Don Miguel Ruiz

Journal Entry

_____

_____

_____

_____

_____

_____

_____

_____

_____

_____

_____

_____

_____

_____

_____

_____

End of the session (Circle one):

🪷 🪷 🪷 🪷 🪷 🪷 🪷 🪷 🪷 🪷
1   2   3   4   5   6   7   8   9   10

Distracted / Unable to drop in   Calm and Relaxed   Connection to Oneness / Bliss

Daily Meditation Log

- Day 1 -

Start of the session (Circle one)

🪷 🪷 🪷 🪷 🪷 🪷 🪷 🪷 🪷 🪷
1   2   3   4   5   6   7   8   9   10

Distracted / Unable to drop in   Calm and Relaxed   Connection to Oneness/ Bliss

Date _____

Time: _____

Duration: _____

Meditation Practice: _____

Posture: _____

"Nothing can harm you as much as your own thoughts unguarded."
— Buddha

Journal Entry

_____

_____

_____

_____

_____

_____

_____

_____

_____

_____

_____

_____

_____

_____

_____

_____

End of the session (Circle one):

🪷 🪷 🪷 🪷 🪷 🪷 🪷 🪷 🪷 🪷
1   2   3   4   5   6   7   8   9   10

Distracted / Unable to drop in   Calm and Relaxed   Connection to Oneness/ Bliss

Daily Meditation Log

Start of the session (Circle one)

1 2 3 4 5 6 7 8 9 10

Distracted / Unable to drop in   Calm and Relaxed   Connection to Oneness/ Bliss

Date _____

Time: _____

Duration: _____

"Hope is praying for rain, but
faith is bringing an umbrella."
— Unknown

Meditation Practice: _____

Posture: _____

Journal Entry

_____

_____

_____

_____

_____

_____

_____

_____

_____

_____

_____

_____

_____

_____

End of the session (Circle one):

1 2 3 4 5 6 7 8 9 10

Distracted / Unable to drop in   Calm and Relaxed   Connection to Oneness/ Bliss

Daily Meditation Log

- *Day 11* -

Start of the session (Circle one)

1 2 3 4 5 6 7 8 9 10

Distracted / Unable to drop in   Calm and Relaxed   Connection to Oneness / Bliss

Date _____

Time: _____

Duration: _____

"There is no other spiritual teacher than your own soul."

— Swami Vivekananda

Meditation Practice: _____

Posture: _____

Journal Entry

_____

_____

_____

_____

_____

_____

_____

_____

_____

_____

_____

_____

_____

_____

End of the session (Circle one):

1 2 3 4 5 6 7 8 9 10

Distracted / Unable to drop in   Calm and Relaxed   Connection to Oneness / Bliss

Daily Meditation Log

Start of the session (Circle one)

🪷   🪷   🪷   🪷   🪷   🪷   🪷   🪷   🪷   🪷
1   2   3   4   5   6   7   8   9   10

Distracted / Unable to drop in   Calm and Relaxed   Connection to Oneness / Bliss

Date _____

Time: _____

Duration: _____

Meditation Practice: _____

Posture: _____

> "Nothing is forever except change."
> — Buddha

Journal Entry

_____

_____

_____

_____

_____

_____

_____

_____

_____

_____

_____

_____

_____

_____

_____

End of the session (Circle one):

1   2   3   4   5   6   7   8   9   10

Distracted / Unable to drop in   Calm and Relaxed   Connection to Oneness / Bliss

Daily Meditation Log

- Day 13 -

Start of the session (Circle one)

   1   2   3   4   5   6   7   8   9   10

Distracted / Unable to drop in   Calm and Relaxed   Connection to Oneness / Bliss

Date _____

Time: _____

Duration: _____

Meditation Practice: _____

Posture: _____

"I will no longer allow anyone to manipulate my mind and control my life in the name of love."
— Miguel Ruiz

Journal Entry

_____

_____

_____

_____

_____

_____

_____

_____

_____

_____

_____

_____

_____

_____

_____

_____

End of the session (Circle one):

   1   2   3   4   5   6   7   8   9   10

Distracted / Unable to drop in   Calm and Relaxed   Connection to Oneness / Bliss

Daily Meditation Log

- Day 14 -

Start of the session (Circle one)

1   2   3   4   5   6   7   8   9   10

Distracted / Unable to drop in   Calm and Relaxed   Connection to Oneness / Bliss

Date _____

Time: _____

Duration: _____

Meditation Practice: _____

Posture: _____

"I understand once again that the greatness of God always reveals itself in the simple things."
— Paulo Coelho

Journal Entry

_____

_____

_____

_____

_____

_____

_____

_____

_____

_____

_____

_____

_____

_____

_____

End of the session (Circle one):

1   2   3   4   5   6   7   8   9   10

Distracted / Unable to drop in   Calm and Relaxed   Connection to Oneness / Bliss

Daily Meditation Log

- Day 15 -

Start of the session (Circle one)

1 2 3 4 5 6 7 8 9 10

Distracted / Unable to drop in   Calm and Relaxed   Connection to Oneness/ Bliss

Date _____

Time: _____

Duration: _____

Meditation Practice: _____

Posture: _____

"It is not in the stars to hold
our destiny but in ourselves."
— William Shakespeare

Journal Entry

_____
_____
_____
_____
_____
_____
_____
_____
_____
_____
_____
_____
_____
_____
_____
_____
_____
_____

End of the session (Circle one):

1 2 3 4 5 6 7 8 9 10

Distracted / Unable to drop in   Calm and Relaxed   Connection to Oneness/ Bliss

Daily Meditation Log

Start of the session (Circle one)

1   2   3   4   5   6   7   8   9   10

Distracted / Unable to drop in   Calm and Relaxed   Connection to Oneness/ Bliss

Date _____

Time: _____

Duration: _____

Meditation Practice: _____

Posture: _____

"If god is all you have, you have all you need."

— John 14:8

Journal Entry

_____

_____

_____

_____

_____

_____

_____

_____

_____

_____

_____

_____

_____

_____

End of the session (Circle one):

1   2   3   4   5   6   7   8   9   10

Distracted / Unable to drop in   Calm and Relaxed   Connection to Oneness/ Bliss

Daily Meditation Log

- Day 17 -

Start of the session (Circle one)

1 2 3 4 5 6 7 8 9 10

Distracted / Unable to drop in   Calm and Relaxed   Connection to Oneness / Bliss

Date _____

Time: _____

Duration: _____

Meditation Practice: _____

Posture: _____

"When you connect to the silence within you, that is when you can make sense of the disturbance going on around you."
— Stephen Richards

Journal Entry

_____

_____

_____

_____

_____

_____

_____

_____

_____

_____

_____

_____

_____

_____

_____

_____

_____

End of the session (Circle one):

1 2 3 4 5 6 7 8 9 10

Distracted / Unable to drop in   Calm and Relaxed   Connection to Oneness / Bliss

Daily Meditation Log

- *Day 11* -

Start of the session (Circle one)

1   2   3   4   5   6   7   8   9   10

Distracted / Unable to drop in   Calm and Relaxed   Connection to Oneness/ Bliss

Date _____

Time: _____

Duration: _____

Meditation Practice: _____

Posture: _____

> "You do not have to struggle to reach God, but you do have to struggle to tear away the self created veil that hides him from you"
> — Paramahansa Yogananda

Journal Entry

_____

_____

_____

_____

_____

_____

_____

_____

_____

_____

_____

_____

_____

_____

_____

_____

End of the session (Circle one):

1   2   3   4   5   6   7   8   9   10

Distracted / Unable to drop in   Calm and Relaxed   Connection to Oneness/ Bliss

Daily Meditation Log

- *Day 11* -

Start of the session (Circle one)

❀ ❀ ❀ ❀ ❀ ❀ ❀ ❀ ❀ ❀
1   2   3   4   5   6   7   8   9   10

Distracted / Unable to drop in   Calm and Relaxed   Connection to Oneness/ Bliss

Date _____

Time: _____

Duration: _____

Meditation Practice: _____

Posture: _____

> "Quiet the mind and the soul will speak."
>
> — Ma Jaya Sati Bhagavati

Journal Entry

_____

_____

_____

_____

_____

_____

_____

_____

_____

_____

_____

_____

_____

_____

End of the session (Circle one):

❀ ❀ ❀ ❀ ❀ ❀ ❀ ❀ ❀ ❀
1   2   3   4   5   6   7   8   9   10

Distracted / Unable to drop in   Calm and Relaxed   Connection to Oneness/ Bliss

Daily Meditation Log

- Day 20 -

Start of the session (Circle one)

1 2 3 4 5 6 7 8 9 10

Distracted / Unable to drop in   Calm and Relaxed   Connection to Oneness / Bliss

Date _____

Time: _____

Duration: _____

Meditation Practice: _____

Posture: _____

"The unexamined life is not worth living."

— Socrates

Journal Entry

_____

_____

_____

_____

_____

_____

_____

_____

_____

_____

_____

_____

_____

_____

_____

_____

_____

End of the session (Circle one):

1 2 3 4 5 6 7 8 9 10

Distracted / Unable to drop in   Calm and Relaxed   Connection to Oneness / Bliss

Daily Meditation Log

Start of the session (Circle one)

1 2 3 4 5 6 7 8 9 10

Distracted / Unable to drop in   Calm and Relaxed   Connection to Oneness/ Bliss

Date _____

Time: _____

Duration: _____

Meditation Practice: _____

Posture: _____

"Be a lamp for yourselves. Be your own refuge. Seek for no other. All things must pass. Strive on diligently. Don't give up."
— Buddha

Journal Entry

_____

_____

_____

_____

_____

_____

_____

_____

_____

_____

_____

_____

_____

_____

_____

_____

End of the session (Circle one):

1 2 3 4 5 6 7 8 9 10

Distracted / Unable to drop in   Calm and Relaxed   Connection to Oneness/ Bliss

You are halfway there!

Seriously—look at you, showing up for yourself day after day. That's no small feat. Keep going—you're building something powerful. The shifts are happening, even if they're quiet.

You've got this!

EMPOWER YOUR PRACTICE:
Plan for your Next Journal!

If you enjoy these tracking pages, continue your practice with six more months of daily pages in the same supportive layout. Order your copy of the *Meditation Companion Journal* now so it arrives before you finish these pages or get a blank journal to continue with.

Meditation Companion Journal

If you've enjoyed the structure of the M4T Journal, this companion journal offers a seamless continuation of the same format. With its clean, simple cover, it feels personal while incorporating the consistency of key design elements from the *Meditation for Transformation Journal.* Inside, you'll find 180+ pages to support six months of continuous practice.

As you approach the end of your current journal, consider ordering the companion journal to keep your practice going. For each journal you complete, use the space on the spine to write the date range for easy reference.

Daily Meditation Log

- *Day 22* -

Start of the session (Circle one)

🪷 🪷 🪷 🪷 🪷 🪷 🪷 🪷 🪷 🪷
1   2   3   4   5   6   7   8   9   10

Distracted / Unable to drop in   Calm and Relaxed   Connection to Oneness/ Bliss

Date _____

Time: _____

Duration: _____

Meditation Practice: _____

Posture: _____

"I am not my thoughts, emotions, sense
perceptions, and experiences. I am not
the content of my life. I am Life. I am the
space in which all things happen. I am
consciousness. I am the Now. I Am."
— Eckhart Tolle

Journal Entry

_____

_____

_____

_____

_____

_____

_____

_____

_____

_____

_____

_____

_____

_____

_____

End of the session (Circle one):

🪷 🪷 🪷 🪷 🪷 🪷 🪷 🪷 🪷 🪷
1   2   3   4   5   6   7   8   9   10

Distracted / Unable to drop in   Calm and Relaxed   Connection to Oneness/ Bliss

Daily Meditation Log

- Day 23 -

Start of the session (Circle one)

🪷	🪷	🪷	🪷	🪷	🪷	🪷	🪷	🪷	🪷
1	2	3	4	5	6	7	8	9	10

Distracted / Unable to drop in   Calm and Relaxed   Connection to Oneness / Bliss

Date _____

Time: _____

Duration: _____

Meditation Practice: _____

Posture: _____

"Character can not be developed in ease and quiet. Only through experience of trial and suffering can the soul be strengthened, ambition inspired, and success achieved." — Helen Keller

Journal Entry

_____

_____

_____

_____

_____

_____

_____

_____

_____

_____

_____

_____

_____

_____

_____

_____

_____

End of the session (Circle one):

🪷	🪷	🪷	🪷	🪷	🪷	🪷	🪷	🪷	🪷
1	2	3	4	5	6	7	8	9	10

Distracted / Unable to drop in   Calm and Relaxed   Connection to Oneness / Bliss

Daily Meditation Log

- Day 24 -

Start of the session (Circle one)

1 2 3 4 5 6 7 8 9 10

Distracted / Unable to drop in   Calm and Relaxed   Connection to Oneness / Bliss

Date _____

Time: _____

Duration: _____

Meditation Practice: _____

Posture: _____

"If you find no one to support you on the spiritual path, walk alone."

— Buddha

Journal Entry

_____

_____

_____

_____

_____

_____

_____

_____

_____

_____

_____

_____

_____

_____

_____

_____

End of the session (Circle one):

1 2 3 4 5 6 7 8 9 10

Distracted / Unable to drop in   Calm and Relaxed   Connection to Oneness / Bliss

Daily Meditation Log

- Day 25 -

Start of the session (Circle one)

1   2   3   4   5   6   7   8   9   10

Distracted / Unable to drop in   Calm and Relaxed   Connection to Oneness / Bliss

Date _____

Time: _____

Duration: _____

Meditation Practice: _____

Posture: _____

"Re-examine all you have been told.
Dismiss what insults your soul."

— Walt Whitman

Journal Entry

_____

_____

_____

_____

_____

_____

_____

_____

_____

_____

_____

_____

_____

_____

_____

End of the session (Circle one):

1   2   3   4   5   6   7   8   9   10

Distracted / Unable to drop in   Calm and Relaxed   Connection to Oneness / Bliss

Daily Meditation Log

- *Day 26* -

Day 26

Start of the session (Circle one)

1   2   3   4   5   6   7   8   9   10

Distracted / Unable to drop in   Calm and Relaxed   Connection to Oneness / Bliss

Date _____

Time: _____

Duration: _____

Meditation Practice: _____

Posture: _____

> "To walk the spiritual path is to continually step out into the unknown."
> — Wallace Huey

Journal Entry

_____

_____

_____

_____

_____

_____

_____

_____

_____

_____

_____

_____

_____

_____

_____

_____

End of the session (Circle one):

1   2   3   4   5   6   7   8   9   10

Distracted / Unable to drop in   Calm and Relaxed   Connection to Oneness / Bliss

Daily Meditation Log

- *Day 27* -

Start of the session (Circle one)

1   2   3   4   5   6   7   8   9   10

Distracted / Unable to drop in   Calm and Relaxed   Connection to Oneness / Bliss

Date _____

Time: _____

Duration: _____

Meditation Practice: _____

Posture: _____

"Be impeccable with your word. Don't take anything personally. Don't make assumptions. Always do your best."

— Don Miguel Ruiz

Journal Entry

_____

_____

_____

_____

_____

_____

_____

_____

_____

_____

_____

_____

_____

_____

_____

_____

End of the session (Circle one):

1   2   3   4   5   6   7   8   9   10

Distracted / Unable to drop in   Calm and Relaxed   Connection to Oneness / Bliss

Daily Meditation Log

- Day 21 -

Start of the session (Circle one)

1   2   3   4   5   6   7   8   9   10

Distracted / Unable to drop in   Calm and Relaxed   Connection to Oneness / Bliss

Date _____

Time: _____

Duration: _____

Meditation Practice: _____

Posture: _____

> "Everything in moderation,
> including moderation."
> — Buddha

Journal Entry

_____

_____

_____

_____

_____

_____

_____

_____

_____

_____

_____

_____

_____

_____

_____

End of the session (Circle one):

1   2   3   4   5   6   7   8   9   10

Distracted / Unable to drop in   Calm and Relaxed   Connection to Oneness / Bliss

Daily Meditation Log

- Day 21 -

Start of the session (Circle one)

🪷 🪷 🪷 🪷 🪷 🪷 🪷 🪷 🪷 🪷
1   2   3   4   5   6   7   8   9   10

Distracted / Unable to drop in   Calm and Relaxed   Connection to Oneness / Bliss

Date _____

Time: _____

Duration: _____

Meditation Practice: _____

Posture: _____

"Happy people build their
inner world; unhappy people
blame their outer world."
— Dalai Lama

Journal Entry

_____

_____

_____

_____

_____

_____

_____

_____

_____

_____

_____

_____

_____

_____

_____

_____

End of the session (Circle one):

🪷 🪷 🪷 🪷 🪷 🪷 🪷 🪷 🪷 🪷
1   2   3   4   5   6   7   8   9   10

Distracted / Unable to drop in   Calm and Relaxed   Connection to Oneness / Bliss

Daily Meditation Log

Start of the session (Circle one)

🪷 🪷 🪷 🪷 🪷 🪷 🪷 🪷 🪷 🪷
1　　2　　3　　4　　5　　6　　7　　8　　9　　10

Distracted / Unable to drop in　　　　Calm and Relaxed　　　　Connection to Oneness / Bliss

Date _____

Time: _____

Duration: _____

Meditation Practice: _____

Posture: _____

"When a person responds to the joys and sorrows of others as if they were his own, he has attained the highest state of spiritual union."
— Lord Krishna

Journal Entry

_____

_____

_____

_____

_____

_____

_____

_____

_____

_____

_____

_____

_____

_____

_____

_____

End of the session (Circle one):

🪷 🪷 🪷 🪷 🪷 🪷 🪷 🪷 🪷 🪷
1　　2　　3　　4　　5　　6　　7　　8　　9　　10

Distracted / Unable to drop in　　　　Calm and Relaxed　　　　Connection to Oneness / Bliss

Daily Meditation Log

- Day 31 -

Start of the session (Circle one)

1 2 3 4 5 6 7 8 9 10

Distracted / Unable to drop in   Calm and Relaxed   Connection to Oneness / Bliss

Date _____

Time: _____

Duration: _____

"All that we are is the result of
what we have thought."

— Buddha

Meditation Practice: _____

Posture: _____

Journal Entry

_____

_____

_____

_____

_____

_____

_____

_____

_____

_____

_____

_____

_____

_____

_____

_____

End of the session (Circle one):

1 2 3 4 5 6 7 8 9 10

Distracted / Unable to drop in   Calm and Relaxed   Connection to Oneness / Bliss

Daily Meditation Log

- *Day 32* -

Start of the session (Circle one)

1	2	3	4	5	6	7	8	9	10

Distracted / Unable to drop in   Calm and Relaxed   Connection to Oneness / Bliss

Date _____

Time: _____

Duration: _____

Meditation Practice: _____

Posture: _____

"I think a spiritual journey is not so much a journey of discovery. It's a journey of recovery. It's a journey of uncovering your own inner nature. It's already there." — Billy Corgan

Journal Entry

_____

_____

_____

_____

_____

_____

_____

_____

_____

_____

_____

_____

_____

_____

_____

_____

_____

End of the session (Circle one):

1	2	3	4	5	6	7	8	9	10

Distracted / Unable to drop in   Calm and Relaxed   Connection to Oneness / Bliss

Daily Meditation Log

- Day 33 -

Start of the session (Circle one)

🪷 🪷 🪷 🪷 🪷 🪷 🪷 🪷 🪷 🪷
1   2   3   4   5   6   7   8   9   10

Distracted / Unable to drop in   Calm and Relaxed   Connection to Oneness / Bliss

Date _____

Time: _____

Duration: _____

Meditation Practice: _____

Posture: _____

> "Accept then act. Whatever the present moment contains, accept it as if you had chosen it. This will miraculously transform your whole life."
> — Eckhart Tolle

Journal Entry

_____

_____

_____

_____

_____

_____

_____

_____

_____

_____

_____

_____

_____

_____

End of the session (Circle one):

🪷 🪷 🪷 🪷 🪷 🪷 🪷 🪷 🪷 🪷
1   2   3   4   5   6   7   8   9   10

Distracted / Unable to drop in   Calm and Relaxed   Connection to Oneness / Bliss

Daily Meditation Log

- Day 34 -

Start of the session (Circle one)

1 2 3 4 5 6 7 8 9 10

Distracted / Unable to drop in   Calm and Relaxed   Connection to Oneness / Bliss

Date _____

Time: _____

Duration: _____

Meditation Practice: _____

Posture: _____

"Your work is to discover your work and then with all your heart to give yourself to it."
— Buddha

Journal Entry

_____

_____

_____

_____

_____

_____

_____

_____

_____

_____

_____

_____

_____

_____

_____

_____

End of the session (Circle one):

1 2 3 4 5 6 7 8 9 10

Distracted / Unable to drop in   Calm and Relaxed   Connection to Oneness / Bliss

Daily Meditation Log

- *Day 35* -

Start of the session (Circle one)

1   2   3   4   5   6   7   8   9   10

Distracted / Unable to drop in   Calm and Relaxed   Connection to Oneness / Bliss

Date _____

Time: _____

Duration: _____

Meditation Practice: _____

Posture: _____

One must still have chaos in
oneself to be able to give birth
to a dancing star."
— Friedrich Nietzsche

Journal Entry

_____

_____

_____

_____

_____

_____

_____

_____

_____

_____

_____

_____

_____

_____

_____

_____

_____

End of the session (Circle one):

1   2   3   4   5   6   7   8   9   10

Distracted / Unable to drop in   Calm and Relaxed   Connection to Oneness / Bliss

Daily Meditation Log

- Day 36 -

1   2   3   4   5   6   7   8   9   10

Distracted / Unable to drop in   Calm and Relaxed   Connection to Oneness / Bliss

Date _____

Time: _____

Duration: _____

Meditation Practice: _____

Posture: _____

> "Peace is the result of retraining your mind to process life as it is, rather than as you think it should be." — Wayne Dyer

Journal Entry

_____

_____

_____

_____

_____

_____

_____

_____

_____

_____

_____

_____

_____

_____

_____

End of the session (Circle one):

1   2   3   4   5   6   7   8   9   10

Distracted / Unable to drop in   Calm and Relaxed   Connection to Oneness / Bliss

Daily Meditation Log

- Day 37 -

1 2 3 4 5 6 7 8 9 10

Distracted / Unable to drop in   Calm and Relaxed   Connection to Oneness / Bliss

Date _____

Time: _____

Duration: _____

Meditation Practice: _____

Posture: _____

"The way is not in the sky.
The way is in the heart."
— Buddha

Journal Entry

_____

_____

_____

_____

_____

_____

_____

_____

_____

_____

_____

_____

_____

_____

_____

End of the session (Circle one):

1 2 3 4 5 6 7 8 9 10

Distracted / Unable to drop in   Calm and Relaxed   Connection to Oneness / Bliss

Daily Meditation Log

- *Day 31* -

Start of the session (Circle one)

1	2	3	4	5	6	7	8	9	10

Distracted / Unable to drop in   Calm and Relaxed   Connection to Oneness / Bliss

Date _____

Time: _____

Duration: _____

Meditation Practice: _____

Posture: _____

"Whenever we hear an opinion
and believe it, we make an
agreement, and it becomes part
of our belief system."

— Miguel Ruiz

Journal Entry

_____

_____

_____

_____

_____

_____

_____

_____

_____

_____

_____

_____

_____

_____

_____

End of the session (Circle one):

1	2	3	4	5	6	7	8	9	10

Distracted / Unable to drop in   Calm and Relaxed   Connection to Oneness / Bliss

Daily Meditation Log

- Day 31 -

Start of the session (Circle one)

1 2 3 4 5 6 7 8 9 10

Distracted / Unable to drop in   Calm and Relaxed   Connection to Oneness / Bliss

Date _____

Time: _____

Duration: _____

"At any moment, you have a choice, that either leads you closer to your spirit or further away from it." — Thich Nhat Hanh

Meditation Practice: _____

Posture: _____

Journal Entry

_____

_____

_____

_____

_____

_____

_____

_____

_____

_____

_____

_____

_____

_____

_____

_____

End of the session (Circle one):

1 2 3 4 5 6 7 8 9 10

Distracted / Unable to drop in   Calm and Relaxed   Connection to Oneness / Bliss

Daily Meditation Log

- Day 40 -

Start of the session (Circle one)

| 1 | 2 | 3 | 4 | 5 | 6 | 7 | 8 | 9 | 10 |

Distracted / Unable to drop in   Calm and Relaxed   Connection to Oneness / Bliss

Date _____

Time: _____

Duration: _____

Meditation Practice: _____

Posture: _____

"She who knows life flows, feels no wear or tear, needs no mending or repair."
— Buddha

Journal Entry

_____

_____

_____

_____

_____

_____

_____

_____

_____

_____

_____

_____

_____

_____

_____

End of the session (Circle one):

| 1 | 2 | 3 | 4 | 5 | 6 | 7 | 8 | 9 | 10 |

Distracted / Unable to drop in   Calm and Relaxed   Connection to Oneness / Bliss

Daily Meditation Log

Start of the session (Circle one)

🪷 🪷 🪷 🪷 🪷 🪷 🪷 🪷 🪷 🪷
1   2   3   4   5   6   7   8   9   10

Distracted / Unable to drop in   Calm and Relaxed   Connection to Oneness / Bliss

Date _____

Time: _____

Duration: _____

Meditation Practice: _____

Posture: _____

"Realize deeply that the present moment is all you have. Make the now the primary focus of your life." — Eckhart Tolle

Journal Entry

_____

_____

_____

_____

_____

_____

_____

_____

_____

_____

_____

_____

_____

_____

_____

_____

_____

End of the session (Circle one):

1   2   3   4   5   6   7   8   9   10

Distracted / Unable to drop in   Calm and Relaxed   Connection to Oneness / Bliss

Daily Meditation Log

Start of the session (Circle one)

| 1 | 2 | 3 | 4 | 5 | 6 | 7 | 8 | 9 | 10 |

Distracted / Unable to drop in   Calm and Relaxed   Connection to Oneness / Bliss

Date _____

Time: _____

Duration: _____

Meditation Practice: _____

Posture: _____

"The deeper the Self-realization of a man, the more he influences the whole universe by his subtle spiritual vibrations, and the less he himself is affected by the phenomenal flux."
— Paramahansa Yogananda

Journal Entry

_____

_____

_____

_____

_____

_____

_____

_____

_____

_____

_____

_____

_____

_____

_____

End of the session (Circle one):

| 1 | 2 | 3 | 4 | 5 | 6 | 7 | 8 | 9 | 10 |

Distracted / Unable to drop in   Calm and Relaxed   Connection to Oneness / Bliss

Chapter 12

Forging Your Own Path

"Be a lamp for yourselves. Be your own refuge. Seek for no other. All things must pass. Strive on diligently. Don't give up."

— Buddha

CONGRATULATIONS! You completed 42 days of meditation! Take a moment to acknowledge just how far you have come. If you missed a day here or there, let it go. If you haven't already, you are on your way to establishing a new habit, and it is time to integrate your practice and make it your own.

As you personalize your practice, use the following prompts to reflect on what was supportive, what tools were helpful, and which ones weren't supportive or helpful. Now is the time to take what works and leave the rest behind!

Reevaluating

Once in a routine, it's easy to become complacent with our posture, surroundings, or practices used. This check-in is a chance to ask yourself: How can my practice better support me? What small changes might help? It's helpful to reflect every few weeks or whenever meditation starts to feel difficult or unfulfilling. Use the questions below to guide you as you establish your personalized practice.

General Observations

What initially drew me to meditation, and has my motivation changed over time?

_____

_____

Am I fully present during meditation, or does it feel like something to "check off" my to-do list?

_____

_____

Am I listening to my body and making physical adjustments to my posture? Is there a way I can sit more comfortably?

_____

_____

Are there particular techniques or styles that resonate with me more than others?

_____

_____

Am I meditating at a time of day that feels natural and sustainable?

_____

_____

How do I feel before and after each session? How has this changed over the past 42 days? What insights do the correlation between my "Before Meditation" and "After Meditation" ratings reveal?

_____

_____

What obstacles tend to disrupt my practice, and how can I address them?

_____

_____

The most rewarding part of my practice is...

What accountability tools have I used (Journal Pages, Habit Tracker)? How have these helped me? How have they limited me?

How do I hold myself accountable? How have I allowed others to be an external support system (meditation partner, account-ability partner, meditation group, M4T Community, etc.)? If I haven't already, would it benefit me to explore these resources for accountability?

Personal Transformation

In what ways has meditation influenced my mindset, emotions, and reactions?

What personal transformation have I experienced over the past six weeks? (e.g., I have more patience; I am more present; I am less stressed.).

_____

_____

How has my connection to my inner world evolved?

_____

_____

How do I integrate mindfulness beyond my formal practice into everyday activities?

_____

_____

What changes—big or small—have I noticed in my relationships, stress levels, or overall well-being?

_____

_____

Looking Ahead

How can I bring more curiosity and openness into my practice?

_____

_____

What aspects of my practice feel stagnant, and how might I refresh them?

_____

_____

Is there a book, teacher, or community that could inspire or challenge me?

_____

_____

Creating Your Practice

As you outline your practice, consider incorporating the following:

How long will my practice be?

What time will I practice each day?

What will my meditation area look like?

What props do I want to incorporate for additional support?

What tools will I continue to use?

What new tools will I explore?

What elements from the journal pages will I continue to use?

What accountability tools will I continue to use?

Will I incorporate a second practice?

What accountability support systems will I continue to use or begin to incorporate (meditation partner, accountability partner, meditation group, M4T Community, etc.)?

Write out your plan:

_____

_____

_____

_____

_____

_____

_____

_____

_____

_____

_____

_____

_____

_____

_____

_____

_____

_____

_____

Revisit Your Commitment Letter

You are on the threshold of a new journey! If it feels supportive for you, reread your commitment letter. If you burned your letter or want to expand on what you wrote, feel free to write another letter and recommit to your practice.

Share the Practice with Others

- **Be an Accountability Partner**: If this journey was transformational for you, you may want to share your experience with others. Consider giving a copy of the *M4T Journal* to a friend and offering to be their accountability person.
- **Start M4T Book Journal Club**: If you have more than one friend you want to engage in the practice, consider starting an M4T Book Club (details in Chapter 5). By supporting others, you may find that your journey is also inspired and enriched.

Keep Exploring!

The *M4T Journal* provides a foundational place to begin, so now is your opportunity to expand and explore. Whatever pulls at you and draws your interest is guiding you on the next leg of the journey. Are you interested in the history and lineages of meditation? Are there other styles and techniques you would like to practice? Are there meditation practitioners or teachers whose style resonates with you? Are you drawn to join a meditation group, a retreat, or a seminar? These are breadcrumbs laid out by your inner guidance. Follow them! If you are looking for a place to start, check out the resources offered in the "Further Reading" section.

Chapter 13

Integrative Transformation

"I am not my thoughts, emotions, sense perceptions, and experiences. I am not the content of my life. I am Life. I am the space in which all things happen. I am consciousness. I am the Now. I Am."

— Eckhart Tolle

Building a daily meditation practice is the ultimate act of self-care, courage, and commitment. Congratulations on integrating your practice and taking the first steps in transforming your life! Take a moment. Savor this part of the journey.

As you continue, some days will be filled with stillness and clarity, and others with restlessness and resistance—but every moment you spend in practice is a step toward greater awareness and transformation. Meditation isn't about perfection; it's about showing up, again and again, with patience, presence, and trust in your inner guidance.

Integrative transformation happens when your meditation practice shifts from an activity you do to the undercurrent of your every thought and action. Watch as it spills into all aspects of your life and becomes a way of being.

As your practice deepens, you'll realize more and more that the wisdom you seek has always been within you. By looking inward

and letting go of beliefs and habits that no longer serve you, you create the transformation you want to see. Trust yourself, trust the process, and know that each breath, each sit, and each moment of stillness is shaping you in profound ways. Keep going, stay curious, and know that every time you return to your practice, you are deepening your connection to your inner wisdom and the world around you.

If you ever find yourself wavering, come back to the tools in this guide. Know that just like you, your meditation practice is ever-changing and growing. You may find that tools that didn't work for you this round may be supportive down the road.

Now is the time to step into your power, start a new narrative, and embody the transformation you seek.

The journey is yours—embrace it fully.

With deep gratitude and joy,

Rebekah Joy Luhrs

Chapter 14

More Journal Pages

"When we strive to become better than we are, everything around us becomes better too."

— Paulo Coelho

How will you continue tracking your sessions? Here are some options:

- **Get a blank notebook or journal:** Use this to write in the individual items you want to keep tracking.

- **Order the *Meditation for Transformation: A Six-Month Journal*:** If you enjoyed the tracking pages in the *M4T Journal*, the *M4T Six-Month Journal* may be the answer. Continue your practice with six more months of daily pages in the same supportive layout—without a repeat of the text in this book. Each journal includes an area on the spine to note the date range, making it easy to track your progress and revisit past reflections.

- **Print blank *M4T Journal* pages:** Download and print blank journal pages using the QR code:

Pay it Forward

Now that you have everything you need to commit to a daily meditation practice, it's time to pass it on and show other seekers where they can find the same support.

Simply by leaving your honest opinion of this book on Amazon, <u>you'll help others find the tools they need to also get started with a daily practice.</u>

If you have found support with this resource, please help spread the word by leaving a review on Amazon, Goodreads, or wherever you found the book!

THANK YOU for making a difference!
Scan the QR code to leave a review:

With deepest gratitude,
Rebekah Joy

References and Credits

- Brewer, J. A., Worhunsky, P. D., Gray, J. R., Tang, Y.-Y., Weber, J., & Kober, H. (2011). Meditation experience is associated with increased cortical thickness and altered default mode network activity. *Proceedings of the National Academy of Sciences, 108*(50), 20254–20259. https://doi.org/10.1073/pnas.1112029108
- Hicks, E., & Hicks, J. (2004). *Ask and it is given: Learning to manifest your desires.* Hay House.
- Hicks, E., & Hicks, J. (2006). *The Law of Attraction: The Basics of the Teachings of Abraham.* Hay House.
- Dispenza, J. (2012). *Breaking the habit of being yourself: How to lose your mind and create a new one.* Hay House.
- Clear, J. (2018). *Atomic habits: An easy & proven way to build good habits & break bad ones.* Avery.

Image Credits

Supporting Resources

**For Additional Meditations, Scan the Code or Follow
the Link**

https://drive.google.com/drive/folders/1aoSMKRu6HCLdBrh3fQRZx
hY4loVqsEes?usp=sharing

For Supporting Resources, Scan the Code or Follow the Link

https://drive.google.com/drive/folders/1ITsgSd2K-
s1XgaBYSx_NJBsZguDEuXgk?usp=share_link

To Access All Meditation Audio Files, Scan the Code or Follow the Link

https://drive.google.com/drive/folders/1aoSMKRu6HCLdBrh3fQRZx hY4loVqsEes?usp=share_link

To Access All YouTube Meditation Videos, Scan the Code or Follow the Link

https://youtube.com/playlist?list=PLUhQH84trrnngb_WK8mnpi97-sbxQrEsd&si=jB2jxCU4PhzD7Msh

Further Reading

History and Lineages of Meditation

Explore the origins, philosophies, and foundational texts that shaped modern meditation practices.

- *An Introduction to Buddhism* **by Peter Harvey -** A comprehensive overview of Buddhist teachings and historical context, this text offers insight into the roots of meditation across different Buddhist traditions.

- *The Mind Illuminated: A Complete Meditation Guide Integrating Buddhist Wisdom and Brain Science for Greater Mindfulness* **by Culadasa (John Yates, PhD) and Matthew Immergut, PhD -** A detailed, step-by-step meditation manual integrating neuroscience and ancient teachings, perfect for anyone wanting to deepen their practice with structure and clarity.

- ***Mastering the Core Teachings of the Buddha: An Unusually Hardcore Dharma Book* by Daniel Ingram -** A bold and practical guide that demystifies enlightenment and challenges traditional ideas about the spiritual path with honesty and depth.

- ***The Way of the Bodhisattva* by Shantideva-** A cornerstone of Mahayana Buddhism, this text outlines the Bodhisattva path, offering profound teachings on compassion, mindfulness, and wisdom as integral aspects of meditation practice. It serves as a foundational work in the Buddhist lineage, guiding practitioners toward altruism and enlightenment for the benefit of all beings.

Yoga Philosophy and Practice

For those looking to integrate meditation into a larger framework of physical and spiritual practice.

- ***The Yoga Sutras of Patanjali* (translated by Swami Sivananda) -** The foundational text of yoga philosophy, this ancient scripture offers teachings on meditation, mindfulness, and the nature of consciousness, providing a roadmap for spiritual growth.

- ***Light on Yoga* by B.K.S. Iyengar -** A classic text for anyone wanting to explore yoga philosophy and its deep connection to mindfulness and meditation. Iyengar's teachings emphasize precision, alignment, and breath in asana practice.

Neuroscience of Meditation

Books that bridge the gap between science and spirituality, offering tools for transformation backed by research.

- ***Breaking the Habit of Being Yourself: How to Lose Your Mind and Create a New One* by Dr. Joe Dispenza** - Combining quantum physics, neuroscience, and biology, this book provides a scientific approach to personal transformation. Dispenza walks you through tools and techniques to rewire the brain and create lasting change.

- ***The Neuroscience of Yoga and Meditation* by Brittany Fair** - A comprehensive exploration of how meditation impacts the brain from a scientific perspective. Ideal for those interested in the growing field of neuroplasticity and meditation.

Spirituality, Consciousness, and Personal Transformation

Support for improving relationships, emotional awareness, and communication.

- ***The Astonishing Power of Emotions: Let Your Feelings Be Your Guide* by Esther and Jerry Hicks** - A practical guide to understanding

emotional guidance and alignment, offering tools to
navigate life with clarity and joy.

- *Autobiography of a Yogi* by **Paramahansa
Yogananda -** A classic spiritual memoir that
chronicles Yogananda's journey from India to the
West, sharing stories of mystical experiences and
timeless yogic wisdom.

- *The Four Agreements: A Practical Guide to
Personal Freedom (A Toltec Wisdom Book)*
by **Don Miguel Ruiz -** A powerful yet simple code
of conduct based on ancient Toltec wisdom. This
book offers four life principles that can transform your
relationships and inner dialogue.

- *A New Earth: Awakening to Your Life's
Purpose* by **Eckhart Tolle -** Tolle offers a
spiritual framework for transcending ego and aligning
with presence. He invites readers to awaken to a
deeper sense of purpose and collective wellbeing.

Practical Meditation and Mindfulness Tools

Books that focus on offering actionable tools for deepening
meditation and mindfulness practice.

- *The Miracle of Mindfulness* by **Thich Nhat
Hanh -** A clear and simple guide to mindfulness
meditation, written by one of the foremost Buddhist
teachers. Hanh offers practical exercises that help
incorporate mindfulness into daily life.

- ***Real Happiness: The Power of Meditation by Sharon Salzberg -*** A practical guide to developing a meditation practice that leads to true happiness. Salzberg offers accessible steps and reflections, focusing on cultivating loving-kindness and mindfulness.

- ***Wherever You Go, There You Are: Mindfulness Meditation in Everyday Life* by Jon Kabat-Zinn, PhD -** A beautifully written introduction to mindfulness meditation that encourages presence and simplicity in daily life. Grounded, practical, and timeless.

Coming Soon!

Meditation Journal: A M4T Companion
by Rebekah Joy Luhrs

If you've enjoyed the structure of the *M4T Journal*, this companion journal offers a seamless continuation of the same format. With its clean, simple cover, it feels personal while incorporating the consistency of key design elements from the *Meditation for Transformation Journal: Tools to Start a Daily Practice and Stick With It!* Inside, you'll find 183 pages to support six months of continuous practice.

As you approach the end of your current journal, consider ordering this companion to keep your practice going. For each journal you complete, simply write the date on the spine for easy reference in the future.

Coming Soon!

Meditations to Ground in the New Earth: Guided Scripts to Awaken the Heart and Expand Consciousness by Rebekah Joy Luhrs

In a time of collective awakening and spiritual evolution, Meditations to Ground in the New Earth offers a sanctuary for those seeking to align with the emerging consciousness of our planet. This collection of guided meditations is designed to help you navigate the shift, grounding your energy and expanding your awareness. Whether you are new to meditation or an experienced practitioner, these guided sessions will support you in staying centered, building your field, and supporting the expansion of our collective evolution.

About the Author

Rebekah Joy Luhrs is a ceremonial songstress and intentional space holder devoted to authenticity, connection, and spirit. As a lifelong seeker, she has explored diverse meditation practices with teachers and communities worldwide. In 2020, she embraced a daily meditation practice—a commitment that profoundly transformed her life. Now, she passionately shares her journey by creating practical tools to support others.

Since 2016, Rebekah Joy has facilitated women's circles, initiations, and retreats. She is an AcroYoga and Thai Massage instructor and the founder of Night Hawk Apothecary.

Currently an artist-in-residence at the OM Sanctuary, Rebekah Joy calls Asheville, NC, home—a place where nature, community, and spirit continue to inspire her work.

Stay Connected!

Newsletter Sign-Up:

Rebekah Joy dedicates her life to embodying Joy, not just as a middle name, but as a birthright. She strives to spread this joy through cultivating authentic connections, holding space, and sharing music that honors the collective experience and the divine. To join in on this co-creation, sign up for her newsletter:

https://substack.com/@rebekahjoyluhrs

Website:

Visit her website for music, meditation, creativity, movement, connection, and so much more!

https://www.rebekahluhrs.com

Social media links:

- https://www.facebook.com/rebekah.luhrs
- https://www.instagram.com/rebekahjoyluhrs
- https://www.youtube.com/@RebekahJoyLuhrs
- https://www.tiktok.com/@rebekahjoyluhrs

Made in the USA
Monee, IL
30 August 2025

23883683R00095